Flashbacks: A Memoir

Flashbacks: A Memoir

Jim Gibbons

Self-published by Author

Kamuela, Hawaii 96743
www.gymgibbons@yahoo.com

Publisher's Note: This is a memoir. Names, characters, places, and incidents are a product of the author's fading memory. Locales and public names are mostly real, unless otherwise mentioned in the *Postscript*. Any resemblance to actual people, living or dead, are sometimes accurate, depending on who you talk to.

Cover photo by Bill Olsen or Bruce Mallon

Book Layout © 2017

Flashbacks: A Memoir 1st ed.
ISBN-13: 9781548459352
ISBN-10: 1548459356

This book is dedicated to my dad,
Robert "Bob" Gibbons
who used to say

"Jim, when are you going to finish something?"

Contents

The Box

I got a birthday present
That made me feel so fine
It was my secret boy-cave
I went there all the time
But people laughed and told me
To wear pants, shoes and socks
Which made me think and ever since
I've thought outside the box

Wake Up, Milwaukee

Christ Milwaukee, wake up
Stop dreaming of beer and bowling
You've been sleeping long enough.
Every year another city drinks you under the table.

What good are you, Milwaukee.
A cow burns down Chicago and you
Can't even get a few square blocks.
Detroit can't stop laughing.

Have you no pride, Milwaukee?
Your Outlaws sport plastic saddlebags
And go the speed limit.
Your rioters shoot blanks and obey curfew.
While National Guardsmen sleep in the park
Your whole city is awake.

Your zoo is full of funny animals
that exit at dusk.
Even your In-Crowd is out of it.
Goodbye Milwaukee, it's been fun.

Goodbye, Milwaukee

My Greyhound Bus ride from Milwaukee to Madison cost one dollar and ninety cents. The date, according to my old journal, was March 24, 1969. Madison was the first leg of my journey to California. I had about a hundred bucks in my wallet and that was it. No bank account, nothing of value, not even my shitty old canvas back pack I toted all over Europe the summer before was worth much.

My reason for leaving Milwaukee was not a vacation, but an escape. I hated the cold winters ever since I froze my nose one night tobogganing in near-zero weather at Smith Park when I was in high school. I recall going down this large slide several times with three or four girls sitting behind me. I sat in front, I guess, because I'm a guy, and none of them wanted to freeze their faces off on the descent.

After the last time one of the girls pointed at me and said, "Your nose is pure white!" I took off my mitten and touched my nose but didn't feel anything. It was numb. I ran into the lodge men's room and looked in the mirror. It was white! I splashed warm water on it until it turned red and started to throb with a burning pain.

A short time later a wart grew on my nose. I'm not saying frostbite was the cause, just that my nose has always been a pain, from hay fever to asthma, sinusitis to rhinitis, and warts! The medicine I used made the wart turn white. It was so embarrassing going to school with a white booger on my nose. As it turned out, the wart came off in a few weeks, but still, once you see someone with a white booger on their nose, that memory will stay with you so that every time you see that person you still see that booger on their nose. I ain't kidding!

But that's not all--it soon started growing back! So I went to a doctor who burned it off. I still remember the awful smell of burning flesh. The result being my nose was a tad smaller and never grew any bigger. You know how older people's noses and ears grow bigger with age? My nose never got any bigger than when I was 16-years old. I'll do the math: 54 years! Yep, a 70-year-old body with a 16-year-old nose.

When I arrived in Madison I called an old fraternity brother, Steve Dilly, who let me crash at his pad before taking off the next day. But the next day was still too cold to hitchhike, so I hung out in the student union, located on the shore of Lake Mendota, a great spot for socializing, and right next to the *Rathskeller*, a German pub on campus! That's right, Madison was the first public university to serve beer on campus, and the drinking age was 18. You can understand why I hung around for a few days.

The second day I ran into Gene Messina, an old high school scholar-athlete friend who led our cross-country team to a City Championship. He joined me and bought a few beers, but Gene was on a bummer, partly because his wife divorced him last year, but mostly because the draft was hanging over him since he was recently reclassified 1-A.

It didn't help when I told him I was drafted in '66, just a few weeks after I dropped a class, leaving me with eleven credits—just one shy of keeping my Student Deferment. I told him about the 7 am physical and how I got my 1-Y with a letter from my allergist, but he didn't have asthma and hay fever or anything wrong with him. Speaking of allergies, that's the other reason I wanted to get out of Wisconsin. Every spring the ragweed and golden rod and other pollens had me sneezing and blowing my nose until it turned red and sore. I'd had enough of that, too!

As much as I liked hanging out, talking to old friends, and drinking beer on campus, I really wanted to head west, and with the relatively cheap bus fare, it was worth not having to stand in the cold for who knows how long. So, I bought a ticket to Iowa City. Why Iowa City? Well, it's just off Highway 80, my main route west, and that's where the University of Iowa is located. I figured that the best place to crash if you don't know anyone is in a college dormitory lounge.

That evening on the Iowa campus I found a dorm, but the entry door was locked, so I waited until a student resident came and I followed him in. He turned and looked at me like "who are you?" I told him I'm meeting Bob in the lobby, which satisfied him and he went to his room. Of course, I didn't know a Bob, but I figured there must be at least one Bob in the dorm. There was no one over by the lounge area so I laid down behind a couch and fell asleep.

The next morning I stuck out my thumb and got picked up by Gary in a Jeep going to Denver. The bad news was his heater was broken and the cloth top was flapping right by my ear, with cold wind blowing on my face. And more bad news: The western sky was grey and once we got out of Iowa we still had the length of Nebraska to drive through, over five-hundred miles before even entering Colorado and heading up to even colder mile-high Denver.

We took turns driving, only stopping for gas and snacks. When we stopped in Ogallala, Nebraska, the headline on the Ogallala Tribune Herald read, "**Ike's Dead**." We talked a bit about our memory of growing up in the fifties, before finally stopping for a real meal in Brush, Colorado called The Skylark Restaurant, which had a woodcut of the Mona Lisa hanging in the lobby. The tag under it read, "$20 -- Call Wayne at 845-2945." Sure enough, and Gary agreed, her eyes followed us across the room.

I picked up the Denver Post and the headline warned, "**Ike's Condition Worsens**," prompting Gary to ask, "What's worse than being dead?" To which I quipped, "Driving through Nebraska in a Jeep with no heater."

When we got to his place in Denver, I was reminded by his roommate that I wasn't even half-way to Frisco—I had forgotten about Utah. He suggested I take a Student Standby flight, so the next day Gary took me to the Denver Airport and I bought a Western Airlines ticket to San Francisco, which according to my old journal, cost $33.60.

I remember coming into the Bay Area on a clear afternoon, seeing the Golden Gate Bridge and then identifying Alcatraz sitting in the middle of

San Francisco Bay. If someone would have told me I'd be sailing my own boat all around that Bay, past Alcatraz to San Francisco, Berkeley, under the Golden Gate Bridge and beyond in the next few years I would have said that's crazy, but it happened.

WHERE'S WALDO?

I had two addresses, one was a friend's brother in San Francisco's Mission District, and the other an old high school acquaintance, Bill Becker, who I'd run into recently at a favorite bar on the East side of Milwaukee called Hooligans, where draft beers were only ten cents. Bill had been visiting family, but was returning to California the next day. He told me to visit him at Waldo Point if I came out. He said it's just north of Sausalito, which is just north of the Golden Gate Bridge. That really encouraged me.

I went to Jimmy's address in the Mission first. He was surprised to see me, of course, since he didn't know I was coming and we hardly knew each other back in Milwaukee, but was nice enough to let me stay in his warehouse until I "found my own pad." The warehouse was an upstairs room with a shower, toilet, FM radio, and a mattress on the floor with two dirty blankets, but for me right then it was perfect. There was also a narrow workbench along the wall with a hot plate, plus a few beakers, and what looked like a Bunsen burner, sort of a makeshift chemistry lab. My guess was he was making LSD, and maybe other drug combinations, but I didn't stick around long enough to find out for sure, although he did ask one favor of me before I left for Waldo Point.

He said he'd give me $20 if I would deliver a package to a house in Oakland. He gave me the name and address, a Kleenex-sized box, wrapped snuggly, and the keys to his '59 Black Cadillac. I was on my way. My directions were to go over the Oakland Bay Bridge and hang a right. I didn't know what was in the box, but I had an idea, and I somehow found the place, parked, and rapped on the door. A black dude opened with a big smile, invited me in and introduced me to a few friends. When

I left and went back to the car I noticed another afro guy sitting shotgun. I had forgotten to lock the doors, but he smiled and treated me like we were old friends. When I asked him if he needed a ride somewhere he said, "No man, I was just digging your car," and got out and said, "Drive safely."

The next day was Sunday and I heard there would be a Be-In at Golden Gate Park, so I had to check it out. Speedway Meadows was packed with long-hairs, which made me a bit embarrassed because my hair was short. When I said goodbye to my Mom before leaving Milwaukee she offered me $20 if I would let her cut my hair. What a deal. The other thing I noticed and mentioned in my journal was that most of these "chicks were braless," not a style very popular in Milwaukee, but definitely had its appeal. After all, what's a better symbol of freedom for women, one that really gets a man's attention, than bouncing braless breasts?

The first band to play was the Shag, which just happened to be a group from Milwaukee I'd seen around campus. They especially stood out because their hair was so long and...shaggy. At one point the crowd separated magically as Hell's Angels on their Harley's rode single-file right down the middle of the grassy field. At some point I had had enough and decided to hitchhike or walk if I had to, over the Golden Gate Bridge to Sausalito and find Waldo Point. Becker said he lived behind an old paddle-wheeler called the *Charles Van Damme.*

The first person I saw behind the paddle-wheeler was a lanky, long-haired blond whose nickname, I would soon learn, was Bitchy Margaret, Bill's old lady. I asked her if she knew a Bill Becker, and she looked at me somewhat unapprovingly, and growled, "Yeah, he's my old man. Follow me." And she climbed onto a rickety old walkway from the parking lot to the *Oakland*, a sunken, but beamy old wooden river boat that once carried potatoes down river to the Bay Area.

As soon as he saw me he smiled and said, "Gibbons, you made it!" I gave him a few highlights of my trip, which made him laugh loudly and say, "Too much!" This phrase was a favorite of his, especially when Maggie would amuse him. Maggie, by the way, was his old lady's preferred name.

He showed me around the old "potato boat," including a shop in the bow that he shared with a boat builder named Greg Baker.

The shop was full of tools, including a band saw, drill press, table saw, chop saw, a lathe, and plenty of work bench space, plus a shower, a gas heater and a narrow bed next to a wood pile in the back where Greg was sleeping until he got his boat livable.

The bathroom was off the kitchen by Nora's bedroom. Nora, a zaftig blond who Maggie met while working at the Post Office in San Francisco, was renting from Bill for $75 a month. She let me leave my back pack in her room, and in our first private conversation asked me, "What's your sign?" When I told her I was a Gemini, she smiled shyly and said, "I always end up fucking Geminis."

This was my first lesson in how astrology can be used to seduce someone. Although I never believed that pseudo-science, I learned that if you want to have sex with someone you must play along. In fact, nine times out of ten, just asking the question is like saying, "I'm willing to have sex with you." The room on top was Bill and Maggie's bedroom, and she also had an "art studio" in the Pilot House.

Bill's project when I arrived was fixing up the "crapper." The bathroom included a round wooden tub, which was big enough to fit six people, a sink, hot water heater, and a two-foot high wooden box with a hole in the top. He explained that they needed a toilet to put up on the box. I asked how he would flush it and he laughed and said the tide comes in twice a day, which makes it "self-flushing."

I spent the first few nights sleeping on a bed in the main room of *Oakland's* stern, which was also the entrance and living area, including the kitchen. Bill and Maggie shared their kitchen and seemed to know a lot of people, many of whom would stop in just about any time of the day or night. Not only was the door never locked, there was no lock on the door.

My second night at about midnight I was woke up by a friend of Maggie's who sat on the bed, explaining that she sometimes slept here when she had a "fight with her old man." Her name was Sheri, and although it was just a single bed, I moved over and let her join me. I had trouble falling back to sleep, and Sheri seemed to be jacked up on something, so we talked for a while, and she told me the best way to fall asleep was to have sex, but quickly pointed out that she was not on the pill so she couldn't help me out. I understood, and though I did have a condom in my wallet, I didn't want to tell her. At one point, I said something that made her laugh, which surprisingly led to hugging and kissing, before her head disappeared under the covers. It didn't take long for her to relieve my angst, and although she got up and made some noise in the kitchen, I slept like a baby.

When Bill said I could crash in his tugboat, *The Loafer*, I was ready for a little privacy. My first time out on the Bay was with Bill in *The Loafer*. We putted over to the Army Corp of Engineers property where he periodically checked to see if there was anything good to salvage, explaining that any flotsam the Army Corp finds they tow over to this beach, which often includes usable lumber and valuable marine equipment.

On my fourth night at Waldo, just before bedtime, Bill told me to come with him to get a toilet. I assumed he bought it or someone gave it to him, so we walked over to the Gate 5 pier, and about half-way to the end sat what looked like a white planter, filled with flowers. Bill turned it over, spilling out the flowers and dirt into the Bay, handed it to me, and whispered urgently, "Let's go!"

I quickly followed him back to the *Oakland* carrying what turned out to be a beautiful ceramic elephant's head toilet. He didn't even tell me till we got back that we stole it, though I was pretty suspicious. Only when Maggie saw it the next day did I find out it belonged to Dan Hicks, who with the Hot Licks, had just come out with one of my favorite songs, "How Can I Miss You When You Won't Go Away."

To sum up my first week in California: I delivered drugs to an Oakland neighborhood in a black Cadillac; I walked over the Golden Gate Bridge without jumping off; I was seduced by astrology and put to sleep by a woman with, I found out later, a jealous, belligerent old man; I sailed out on the Bay for the first time; and stole a toilet from a famous musician. And that was just for starters!

A few of Sausalito's more notable characters lived on the waterfront aboard the 1880s ferryboat *Vallejo*. Alan Watts, author of international renown who held fellowships from Harvard and was widely recognized for his Zen writings, resided on the west end. His side was sparsely furnished and lacked color and visual stimuli—strictly a place for meditation.

Alan Watts Befriends Me

My FIRST FEW WEEKS LIVING at Waldo Point made me realize that I wasn't going anywhere else anytime soon. I liked hanging out on the Sausalito waterfront, meeting Becker's friends and neighbors, mostly boat people, and partying on the back deck of his old sunken potato boat almost every afternoon. When he was ready to party he'd say, "Gibbons, let's prime the pump!" This meant the first beer will get us going the way a little water will prime one of those *Portagee* hand pumps.

Usually a few others had already arrived, maybe with a guitar and a six-pack, or willing to walk over to the Bait Shop and buy more beer. Sometimes he'd just crank up the music on KSAN, which blasted out the back door, alerting the neighbors that it's party time.

But I needed a place of my own, a little privacy, and to do that I needed a job. I applied at the Tides Bookstore and the Sausalito Post Office, which required a written test, and depending on your score could take anywhere from one to three months before they hired you. But I was broke now. I was down to my last dollar, and though I pretty much knew what I wanted to spend it on, I remembered the example my high school Sociology teacher used to show us unworldly students how low some people will go by spending their last dollar on alcohol. So, I thought for a minute…what would be the best way to spend my last dollar? Open a bank account? Invest in the stock market? Donate to charity? That just brought me back to my original choice—a cold beer!

On my way to spending my last dollar on alcohol, I ran into Greg Baker, Bill's shop mate, who told me an artist named Jean Varda, aka Yanko, needed someone to do clean-up work in his studio and will pay $2 an hour. Two dollars an hour was what the bookstore paid, which was normal for a service job in 1969.

Greg went on to explain that Yanko shared a houseboat with Alan Watts, called the *Vallejo*, which was docked at Gate 3.

This was the real Alan Watts! He introduced the beat counter-culture to Eastern philosophy with books like *East Meets West, The Way of Zen, Beat Zen, Square Zen*, and many more. I especially liked haiku poetry, which I believe he, along with Gary Snyder, Kenneth Rexroth, and Phillip Whalen, to name a few, helped popularize here in the west.

So, Greg took me over and introduced me to Yanko, already in his seventies, but spry and willing to show me his cluttered studio, with scraps of colorful cloth and paper scattered all over the floor and on his paintings. His main thing was collage, sticking these scraps onto painted plywood sheets of different colors and sizes to make seascapes, village scenes of women adorned in colorful clothes, and a few unfinished pieces that looked more like, according to my old journal, "...a 6th grade art class project."

I didn't know at the time how impressive his artistic background was. Born in Greece, but moved to Paris where he roomed with Braque and Miro, just two names I remember from my college Art History class. Had a one-man show in London in 1929 that was so successful he claimed, "From then on I lived on my painting."

He moved to southern France and was frequently visited by numerous artists, including Pablo Picasso. In 1939 he came to New York for a one-man show that sold out! The next year he got a studio in Hollywood, eventually moving up the coast to Monterey and Big Sur, where Henry Miller came to hang out for a few weeks before he found his own place and wrote his *Tropic of Sex* trilogy. Then in the early '50s came to Sausalito and bought the *Vallejo*. Watts came on board ten years later.

Varda told me I could start tomorrow morning at 9 o'clock, so suddenly spending my last dollar on a beer became a celebratory act that even my old Sociology teacher would no doubt approve of.

The next day I showed up on the *Vallejo* on time and spent the morning picking up and cleaning up after him, while he put the finishing touches on a collage that looked like a woman wearing a peacock on her head. I met his house girl, a young blond, whose name I forget, who seemed to come and go with the tide, her long maxi-dress swishing behind her like a wave.

Lunch was something else, with people from all over stopping by with wine and cheese, sharing stories of their worldly adventures, and according to my journal from April 17, which was my very first day, I mention that we had four bottles of wine between seven of us.

Yes, I got to eat with him and his guests, mostly artists and writers who lived in the Bay Area and down along the California coast. When Yanko was ready for his nap, people politely said adieu and left. My next job was to stand outside on the back deck and make sure nobody bothered him while he was napping. Tough job but someone had to do it.

The best part of this job was when Alan Watts, who lived in the forward half of the old ferryboat, would come out during his "writing break" and chat. Said he was working on several projects, one being his autobiography (*In My Own Way*), and a looming deadline on the intro to his book of essays on man's relation to the material world (*Does it Matter?*).

I mentioned that I read a few of his essays in *Playboy* magazine, which elicited a grin, saying he liked and respected "Hef" and what he's accomplished with his "intellectual girlie magazine." And yes, they would be included in his book of essays.

We usually talked about local stuff, or the smog you could see across the Bay on days when the wind died down. This was before lead was taken out of gasoline. He'd complain about the smog between puffs on his fancy old pipe that was *not* filled with marijuana, even though he liked his experience smoking pot and taking LSD. He said because pot was illegal he and Varda agreed that no pot should be smoked on the *Vallejo*.

He felt psychedelics helped "induce the mystical experience and users are entitled to some constitutional protection." He was angry he couldn't continue research in the field and called it a "barbarous restriction of spiritual and intellectual freedom." I couldn't have said it better.

I made $38 in three days, and was offered to stay on the *Stuart and Jeanne*, a small houseboat anchored out on Richardson Bay, which included a skiff to row back and forth to shore. Here's a quote from my journal from early May: "Been on the *Stuart and Jeanne* for three days. Life is good. Got laid twice in the last three days! And get this—to Norma Riddle and Nora Riddell.

Norma has a houseboat anchored nearby, who I got to know a little better when I heard a muffled scream the other night. I jumped out of bed and went out on deck to see her standing on her stern watching her little rowboat float slowly toward Strawberry Point. I jumped in my skiff and rowed after it, brought it back to her boat, and she thanked me by inviting me in for some hot tea, then rewarded me for my chivalry with..."

Rather than finish this journal quote, I'll let the reader's imagination run wild, and move onto Nora Riddell, Bill's tenant on the *Oakland*, who got me high on LSD, and according to my journal was "not that enjoyable. I didn't feel very sexy and let her do most of the work. I just want to be her friend, not her lover. I should just stick to beer and pot."

By the end of May, Varda said he "didn't need my services anymore," which was fine with me because I had fifty bucks in my pocket, a free boat to live on, and figured I'd be hearing from the Post Office or the Tides any day.

Then Jeanne showed up and wanted to move back on her boat again, said she had broken up with Stuart. No problem, as Becker had recently acquired a 22-foot steel lifeboat that he'd sell for $100. I gave him a twenty for a down payment and became the owner of a boat I jokingly named *Cowpie*.

Everything seemed to be happening with perfect timing. A week or so before Jeanne returned, Becker heard there was a finger dock floating in Richardson Bay after a big storm. We jumped in his tug boat, found it, and towed it back, replacing the old rickety walkway with a floating dock that connected the parking lot to the *Oakland*. I tied the *Cowpie* to one of the fingers, and now I had easy access to live and work on it.

Then on June 6th I started working at the Sausalito Post Office. I was on the night shift, from 2am to 10am, which gave me the daytime to work on my boat, and I could still party at night if I wanted to, but getting enough sleep then became my biggest problem. I had worked the graveyard shift in Milwaukee at the American Can Company back in '66 while taking a full load at UW-Milwaukee, so I knew what to expect—less sleep.

RICKY WATTS

What I didn't expect was Watts showing up at the Tides Bookstore about a year later with a clean looking 16-year-old blond he introduced to me as his son, Ricky. I should mention that I lasted ten weeks at the Post Office before they fired me for not shaving my beard or cutting my hair. It's even mentioned in my termination letter. A few months after losing the Post Office job I got hired at the Tides Bookstore.

Alan asked me if I'd show Ricky around and introduce him to some of my waterfront friends. I hadn't even seen Watts more than once in the past year and now suddenly he introduces me to his son as if we're old friends? Fact is, Alan hardly knew anyone on the waterfront. He knew people of different cultures all over the world, but the best friend he could come up with where he'd been living for the past ten years was me? Suddenly we're old pals?

I agreed to take Ricky with me after my shift, which was almost over, so Alan thanked me and disappeared, while Ricky browsed around the bookstore waiting for me. Turned out Ricky's mom back east sent him to his estranged father because he had gotten into some trouble, typical teenage rebellion stuff, as I recall. He seemed like a nice enough kid, but I really didn't like feeling responsible for him, I didn't want to be his surrogate dad or even his friend.

We went down to the Gates and ran into a few people I knew hanging out in the Ark parking lot. These were not the type of guys a parent would want their child to befriend, but what was I supposed to do? There weren't any kids his age living at the Gates that I knew, and since these guys were being real nice to him I figured my job was done.

Over the next several months, every time I'd see Ricky he looked a little funkier, as if he hadn't changed his clothes or combed his stringy hair since that first day. I was particularly bothered by some of the guys I saw him with I knew were either alcoholics or drug addicts. Two names come to mind, Peacock and Toothless Tom. I'm quite sure that they befriended him because he had money. Yes, my other guess was Alan gave him an ample allowance to get him off the boat so he could finish writing his autobiography.

Then one day I was hanging out in the *Ark* parking lot with some of the guys when Ricky drove up in a brand new pick-up truck with a new chainsaw in the bed. He got out and nodded to us as he quickly walked toward the cluster of houseboats. As soon as he was out of sight, one of the guys, let's call him Jeremy, walked over to Ricky's truck, and with a big smile on his face, picked up the chainsaw, walked over to an old junked Chevy coup and stuck it in the trunk, then leaned against it as if nothing happened. The others grinned, as if this was so clever, but it pissed me off and I said, "That's fucked up," as I walked away. I felt guilty that I didn't stick around and make sure he gave it back, which I found out much later he never did.

I first met Jeremy Conn in January of 1971 when he stopped at Waldo Point to see his friend Buck Knight on the way to British Columbia to start grad school…but he never left. He was an Irishman from Connecticut who went from being a U.S. Army translator to a Uconn college grad to a waterfront drunk. But let him tell it.

"Most people have a few drinks and that's it, but I turned into The Hulk, Mr. Hyde, Green Slime. My body would go on when my conscious mind shut down…black out…no off-switch."

I remember late one night he was yelling really loud over and over again, "COON! COON! COON!" Turned out a new guy moved into a houseboat near him and his name was Jeremy Coon. So, like Nora Riddell and Norma Riddle, now we had a Jeremy Conn and a Jeremy Coon. In the daytime when Conn was sober there was no problem, but that night was an example of "no off-switch."

Jeremy continued his uncontrollable drunken behavior until 1977, when he finally realized he needed help, and started going to AA meetings. He credits Alcoholics Anonymous with helping him stay sober, and hasn't had a drink since.

Jeremy and I became friends over the years, before and after he was sober, and then in 2014 I decided I wanted to write about the waterfront and emailed him. In one email I mentioned the chain saw episode and how it bothered me for years. He told me he went to an AA meeting a few years ago, and running the meeting was Ricky Watts.

"I went up to him and told him what I had done and offered to make restitution. He laughed and said if I spoke at his meeting we could call it even. It took the burden off my back. I love AA."

I don't recall seeing Ricky or his dad after that. Jean Varda died in January of '71, I left the waterfront for Mendocino County in the late summer of that year, and Alan Watts died in '73.

I would like to leave you with a quote from the first chapter of Watts' book of essays (*Does It Matter?*) that sheds a little light on his darker side, or his prescient prediction of the near future that he called a "reasonably certain guess." Keep in mind this was written nearly fifty years ago!

"In the year of Our Lord Jesus Christ 2000, the United States of American will no longer exist. Why? Because the land and its life can now so easily be destroyed by the sudden and catastrophic methods of nuclear or biological warfare, or any combination of insidious means as overpopulation, pollution of the atmosphere, contamination of the water and erosion of our natural resources by maniacal misapplication of technology. For good measure, add the possibilities of civil and racial war, self-strangulation of the great cities and breakdown of all transportation and communication networks. And that will be the end of the USA, in both senses."

On the other end of the *Vallejo*, the stern, lived Jean Varda, a Greek collage artist who was the yang to Watts' yin. Varda's side of the boat was a riot of color, sculptures, paintings, food, wine, music, and people. Varda lived for celebration. He was known internationally for his art, which he created from dresses and clothing purchased from the Sausalito Salvage Shop. Varda died in '71, Watts in '73. The *Vallejo* is still on the waterfront, preserved as a memorial to two great philosophies of life.

Smog

Smog all around us
Choking Mt. Tam and the people in the city
Robbie says it's like a burning house
Flames on all sides
but we're safe down here
with our noses at sea level
But Ebbie won't buy it
He drags the day around like a new disease
"Look at it! That's why I'm going back
to WisCONsin."

Me with my tall bicycle that Ebbie put together with an old bike frame.

Bicycle

Ebbie built this bicycle.
I thank Heather for the fine paint job.
People smile and point when I ride by.
You see, it's twice the height of a normal bike
with a view those shorties lack.
Some think it takes special skill to ride
Or figure there's a trick up my handlebars.
They often stop me and ask,
"How do you do it?"
Not usually being in any kind of hurry
I show them.

Ebbie reading a book.

Working At the Tides Bookstore

Listening to KSAN
A few rain refuges browsing
Sitting on the stairs reading
Suddenly Ron Martin walks in smiling
Pokes a bottle of Hennessy in my face
We drink...I have mine with coffee
Ron's probably the only person
Kicked out of both the No Name Bar
and Mt. Tamalpais for life!
He says Mim is the only person who loves him
And laughs about his recent bout with depression
Ending with a night at the opera
Where he admits he was getting obnoxious
Before being asked to leave the theater
He smiles "Can you imagine
            a drunken hippie
            on a bummer
            at the opera?"

Sex, Drugs, and Poetry?

I WAS WORKING AT THE Tides Bookstore in the spring of 1970 when my book came out. I had been a Milwaukee Poet, and with my friend Chuck put out a little poetry magazine we called Pretty Mama, using the English department's version of a copy machine. The best part was probably the cover, always eye-catching art done by my wife Lois. It was through the magazine I met Ed Burton.

Ed had obtained an old letterpress that he planned to restore in his basement, and invited me over to check it out. He had seen Pretty Mama and asked if he could print a future issue once he got his press working. When he did, he named it Morgan Press, after his six-year-old daughter, and Pretty Mama was the first thing he printed.

It was such an improvement we thought about selling it at the local Head Shop, but Lois and I had gone to Europe that summer (1968), and when we returned I sort of dropped out of the poetry scene, though I was still writing and visiting Ed occasionally. Since I didn't want to do Pretty Mama any more, and Chuck had graduated and moved back home to Upper Michigan, Ed continued with some of the same poets, but changed the name to Hey Lady.

My brief marriage to Lois broke up (in retrospect I blame myself), and after refusing to go to class at the beginning of the spring semester to fin-ish my BA in English, I finally decided to head for California. There were numerous reasons, but I liked telling people it was because of a popular TV ad for an allergy medicine that gave the viewer two choices to relieve the suffering: I) Take an ocean voyage, or 2) Take Allerest. I chose a version of the first one.

The waterfront was heaven for my sinuses. I could breathe through both nostrils most of the time, and since I'd quit sneezing and coughing up phlegm, I would forget about my allergies until I returned to Wisconsin for visits. I remember once driving over the Mississippi River from Iowa to Wisconsin and sneezing for the first time in months--"ACHOO!!!" *Oh yeah, I have hay fever.*

I missed my friends and family back in Wisconsin, but Becker and I were not the only ones from Milwaukee. Besides Becker there was Ed Hantke, known as Ebbie, one of the earlier anchor-outs who loved working on anything mechanical, but mostly seemed to like doing nothing. We often did nothing together. I'd stop over for coffee in the morning, then we'd hop in his outrigger canoe and paddle to shore, maybe go for a bike ride along Gate 5 Road, stopping to chat with people he knew, which seemed to be everybody.

When I needed a bicycle, Ebb took an old frame, turned it upside down, welded on support pieces, and extended the seat and handle bars. Whenever I would ride into Sausalito tourists would snap photos of this hippie on his weirdly tall bicycle. (see photo and poem)

My book, *Prime the Pump*, was mostly poems I had written in Milwaukee, some of which embarrassed me, but others I still like, especially the ones I wrote on my boat. I was really pleased to have my own book, and since Ed did it as a *Labor of Love*, I just gave it away to my new friends on the waterfront. I did, however, give the Tides some copies to sell. I still remember coming to work one day and there in the window was a display of my books. It certainly was a pleasant surprise, made all the more surprising because they didn't tell me they were planning to do that.

Now I was known around the waterfront as a poet, and among the people who gave me positive feedback was Shel Silverstein. I didn't really know Shel, but one day I was leaving work with a few books in my hand when I ran into Shel on his way to the No Name Bar. I stopped him, introduced myself, told him how much I liked *A Boy Named Sue*, the hit song he wrote for Johnny Cash, and gave him my book. A week or so later I saw him again and he told me how much he enjoyed it, and invited me over to his boat for a get together with a few other local writers.

This was a chance for me to meet other writers and perhaps advance my literary career, but on the way over that afternoon I ran into Sparky, a frizzy blond with inviting eyes and perky breasts under a see-through blouse that mesmerized my libido and made me forget where I was going.

She said she had some really good mescaline, and a few hours later we were at a friend's cabin on Mt. Tam making waves on a water bed. Yeah, I know, I missed out on a rare opportunity to meet other writers, but what was I supposed to do? I just couldn't turn down this sweet flower child's kind offer to share a tab of mescaline? That's just not the way I rolled.

Then a few days later, I really don't remember if it was days or weeks, I saw Shel walking toward his boat with Bill Cosby. I'm not saying Cosby would have been there the day I was invited to join the group, but just that I can't believe I turned down a genuine invite by Shel Silverstein because of a hippie chick. Yeah, sure, Sparky and I had fun, but that kind of fun was becoming common place, and to this day, not going to Shel's boat is still way up on my long list of regrets. If I had a *regret-o-meter,* it would be right up there with…oh, there's so many. Forget I mentioned it.

I should mention that Bill was friends with another Milwaukeean named Bill Olsen aka Olie. Olie also knew Ed Burton, and one of his hobbies was photography. He and his girlfriend Meryl came out to visit during Christmas vacation. His photos of the waterfront scene were in my book, and Ed chose one of Greg Baker for the cover. Greg liked to dress like a 19th Century Navy Captain, and he wore his military outfit for that photo.

Greg became my self-appointed mentor. Besides helping me get that job at Varda's when I was down to my last dollar, he lent me books to read, helped me in the shop, and sold me an 8-foot dory he built himself, for just $50. One of my favorite books of Greg's was *Sailing Alone Around the World* by Joshua Slocum. When I mentioned the book to Becker, he said, "I want to sail around the world and NOT write a book about it. Haha." I recall telling Becker I wanted to write a book called *Sailing Alone Around Angel Island*.

It was Christmas Day of 1969 when I first sailed the Cowpie. Here's a quote from my journal: "Well, I told myself I'd sail by Xmas and sure enough it happened. I found a 9 X 12-foot tarp in a vacated Xmas tree lot and used it as a square sail. Olie, Meryl, Bill and I sailed away in a perfect west wind under a beautiful blue sky...only problem was we couldn't come about, so I threw my new Danforth mud anchor overboard and now I'm anchored out near Clipper Harbor. They all jumped in my little dory and rowed back to shore. I chose to stay with the boat. Only problem is, now I don't know how I'll get back to the dock."

Bay Morning

It's morning
I toss open my hatch cover
Breathe thru both nostrils and yell
EEEEEEEAAAAAAHHH!!!
Seagulls continue their usual noise
Fog rolls thru the Golden Gate
Cloud halo over Mt. Tam
Blue ski straight up
Think I'll visit Ebbie for breakfast
He'll smile and say
"Climb aboard and have some cawfee."

Mast

Got my new mast today
Greg, Roy, Babi and me
Dropped it right through my cabin roof.
Shrouds, turnbuckles, and
All the rigging is on too.
Makes *Cowpie* look like a real sailboat.
And what's more
You can't tell from the outside
It's planted smack in the middle
of my bed.

On the Recent Visit of My Friend Dave Porter

Just him and me sailing across the Bay
Laughing and getting drunk on Red Mountain wine.
My eyes on the Golden Gate Bridge
His still on Mt. Tamalpais.
Me shouting orders,
    "Pull in the fucking jib sheet
    and pass that bottle!"
But he gets serious and spins around,
    "It's nice being out here in the middle of things
    instead of always on the edge."

Barter

Down here at Waldo
we practice a little thing called barter.
It means getting what you want for nothing.
Might go like this: I find a toilet seat on Strawberry Beach.
Greg gives me a brass snap shackle.
Joe scores some stainless-steel cable.
I tell him I could use some cable about that size.
He likes my old fashion school desk,
the one Peter gave me for helping pour
concrete ballast in his lifeboat.
I offer my toilet seat. He grins,
"Take fucking cable and owe me something."

Next day I'm giving some fresh Gemini lady
a tour of the Cowpie
when what's-his-grin sails up in the Shark.
Eyes bigger than usual, one lands on the school desk
the other on fresh lady.
I'm ready to give him back his cable
when he swoops up my brass snap shackle,
"Hey Gibbons, just what I needed!"
We laugh and call it even.

Sailing Backwards

Keel in the mud off Clipper Harbor.
Tide still going out.
Joe Tate sails by in the Shark
Tells me to hoist my jib
And sail out backwards.
Anchor up…jib flying…I'm free!
I raise my mainsail and head toward
Strawberry Point.
I'll drop anchor with full sail
Set *Cowpie* for another night.
Give us plenty of water
And a new neighborhood.

Bottom Job

Scraping my hull on Baily's barge
through copper bottom paint
down to bare medal.
Copper dust in my face.
Roy's mask for protection.
SCRAPE! SCRAPE!
Peter insists it must all come off.
Bill says just the loose stuff.
Steve suggests the electric grinder.
Greg tells me to do the best I can.
Bob helps me scrape.

Sailing the *Cowpie* to San Francisco

ONE OF THE MORE INTERESTING women I met anchored out was Diane Allen from Memphis, Tennessee. I was enchanted by her southern accent, and I couldn't resist her dimpled smile. She taught classes on how to interpret your dreams. I remember telling her in our first *dream* conversation, "The only dreams I remember are *wet dreams*...how do you interpret that?"

She laughed, and told me maybe I needed a girlfriend. She continued, as if I was one of her students. "Write them down when you first wake up, before you get out of bed. Have a pen and paper handy..." and she paused, giving me that dimpled smile, "...and maybe a Kleenex to wipe up the mess." We both laughed.

The first night I stayed with her on her boat, sure enough I woke up in the early hours to find her writing in her notebook. "Have any good dreams last night?" I yawned. She turned toward me and answered with, "Did you?" I told her I dreamt I was sleeping in my mother's womb, but wanted to crawl out of the wetness and on to dry land. To which she wondered if I thought floating on the water felt like being in the womb? Then wondered if babies in the womb snore?

One day she told me her aunt just got engaged to a well known character actor named Henry Jones, and they were having an engagement party in San Francisco. Did I want to go?

I'd been wanting to sail the *Cowpie* over to Frisco, and this seemed like the perfect time, so I suggested we sail over on my boat. She liked that idea, so a few days later we sailed across the Bay, anchored the *Cowpie* in Aquatic

Park, rowed to shore in my 8-foot dory that I always towed behind, pulled it up on the beach, and walked to her aunt's party.

It turned out to be in a top floor penthouse that had an awesome view of the Bay. This was classy stuff for a Milwaukee farm boy, and the obvious truth was that I really looked and felt out of place, with my long hair and beard, not to mention my flannel shirt, torn jeans and sockless tennis shoes.

She introduced me to her aunt and her aunt's fiancé, and I realized I had seen his face in more than a few movies and TV shows. He was usually the saloon keeper or the store clerk in old westerns. I should add a photo of him to go with this article…better yet, if you're interested just go to Wikipedia.

Since I didn't know anyone, and Diane was talking to her aunt, I walked over to get a better look from the north facing living room windows. I could see the Golden Gate Bridge, Alcatraz, Angel Island, and Aquatic Park—and there was my boat, the only boat anchored in Aquatic Park. I was so excited to see my boat down there I turned to show Diane, but instead this tall fellow introduced himself as Art Hoppe.

Before it dawned on me that he was the Art Hoppe who wrote a daily column for the San Francisco Chronicle, I pointed to the *Cowpie* and told him, all proudly, "We just sailed over on my boat." That seemed to pique his interest, and the ensuing conversation kept returning to me and my lifestyle and what it was like living anchored out on a small boat, and hanging out with the other "waterfront misfits…I mean artists," and he laughed. It was almost like he was interviewing me for a future satirical column.

No doubt what stood out the most in my conversation with Hoppe was his laugh, sort of a machine gun ha-ha-ha-ha-ha-ha-ha-ha, going up and down the musical scale. It sounded like the Great Gildersleeve's laugh on that old 50s radio show, and if you remember that, you're older than me.

After a few drinks and getting a few more unapproving looks from a few of the more snobbish guests, I told Diane it was time to go. The most important thing to keep in mind when sailing a boat without a motor is to know the tide table, which was printed in a little blue booklet that I always carried with me.

We had to leave Sausalito on the outgoing tide, but by the time the Golden Gate Bridge came into full view the tide was turning, the west wind was picking up, and soon we were sailing all of 4 knots, about as fast as the *Cowpie* was meant to go.

Keep in mind that steel life boat hulls were not built for speed, but for safety, and they are double-ended for protection from oncoming waves. To make the *Cowpie* even slower, I may have put too much ballast in my bilge. Then I added another cabin for headroom, a woodstove for heat and cooking, not to mention all the rigging and two anchors. It added up to slow sailing.

Whenever I was in the doldrums with not much wind, my old canvas sail would sag, and the boom would have to be secured. I would get out my huge oar called a sweep, set it in an oarlock on the stern's gunnel, and scull in sweeping motions. That was a hell of a workout, but saved me from a few close calls.

We said goodbye and headed back to the boat. The tide was still coming in so I decided to return in a counter-clockwise circle around the east side of Alcatraz and Angel Island, and hopefully catch the outgoing tide by the time we hit Raccoon Straits, between Angel Island and Tiburon.

We got fairly close to Alcatraz, and could see some of the American Indian occupiers watching, a few waving at us By the time we got around Angel Island and into Raccoon Straits we got caught in a rip current, where the incoming tide meets the outgoing tide, making for violent choppy waters and nearly impossible to control the boat.

To make matters worse, we had to tack into the west wind, and we weren't really making any progress, but soon the outgoing tide took over and we made it around the Tiburon Peninsula and back to Richardson Bay before dark.

A few days later, no doubt inspired by Art Hoppe and a few of the snooty guests, I wrote the following poem, *Mud.*

Mud

Unable to row out to my boat at low tide
I sit on the finger dock and look at the mud.
The people on the hill find mud
dirty and disgusting.
They tell me it stinks just awful.
I listen without argument.
How do you tell people with scented bathrooms
that mud just smells different?
How can I explain mud to those who think
Marine toilets will Save the Bay?
How can I carry on a good mud conversation
with people who have looked down so long on mud
they've even forgotten how good it feels
between the toes?

Bad dog walking in the mud at low tide

My Escape from Alcatraz

I WAS ONLY ON ALCATRAZ Island once and it wasn't off a tour boat and it wasn't to compete in the Escape from Alcatraz Triathlon. And no, in case my grandchildren are reading this, I didn't do time there when it was a prison from 1934 to 1963, or play a prisoner in any of the Alcatraz movies. My trip happened back in the late spring of '71 when the American Indians were occupying The Rock, as they liked to call it. Here's a quick review:

In November of 1969 three boats took members of twenty tribes from all over the country to occupy Alcatraz, reclaiming it as "Indian land and demanding fairness and respect for Indian Peoples." The spokesman for the Indians was a Mohawk from New York named Richard Oakes, who offered the U.S. Government "$24 in glass beads and red cloth." Oakes said, "We hold The Rock," and that became the movement's motto.

Tragically, a few months later his 13-year-old daughter fell from a three-story structure in the prison and died. He and his wife left the Island shortly after, as did many others during the 18-month occupation.

Grace Thorpe, daughter of Jim Thorpe, the first Native American to win Olympic gold (1912), was one of the occupiers who helped convince celebs like Jane Fonda, Antony Quinn, Marlon Brando, Jonathan Winters, Buffy Sainte-Marie, and Dick Gregory to visit the Island to show their support. Creedance Clearwater Revival gave $15,000 for a boat they named Clearwater for more reliable transport.

But by the spring of '71 most occupiers were gone and many that were left wanted off, too. There had been numerous power struggles among the various tribes almost from the beginning, and the fact that they lasted 18 months seemed victory enough, although Uncle Sam said, if I may paraphrase, *Sorry Injuns, but Alcatraz is not yours to reclaim, so beat it!*

I knew the protest had waned over the months, as most original occupiers were students who went back to school or those with jobs and a real life had to get back to their routines, leaving mostly drug addicts and homeless hippies on the Island. But they needed supplies, and they needed a boat. I don't know what happened to the Clearwater, I never saw it in Sausalito. I'd occasionally see a few Indians hanging out at the Gates looking for someone to take them out to the Island, and a few sympathetic locals did, but mostly just to get them out of the neighborhood.

Then one day my friend Jack asked me if I'd like to make $100. A hundred bucks back then was good money. I had been working part-time at the local bookstore for $2 an hour, so $100 to me was the equivalent of 50 hours of work! "Hell yeah," I replied.

He told me the U.S. government had cut off all electrical power and phone service to the Island, so the remaining occupiers on had cut and stripped the prison of copper wire, which had gone up to $1 a pound, and they needed a boat to bring it to shore.

Jack had a tugboat called the No.1 and he knew I had just purchased a 30-foot steel lifeboat from a guy who claimed he had an epileptic seizure on the boat and refused to spend another night aboard. He just wanted to get the hell out of there, and I happened to be the first person he saw when coming to shore, so he sold it to me cheap, right on the spot, then tossed his back pack on his shoulder and split. I never saw him again.

I knew what we planned to do was a federal crime, but it didn't really bother me. What could happen? So, within a few days Jack fired up his ancient one-cylinder diesel engine (chug-a-chug-a-chug) and we towed my lifeboat out to the Island. As we approached the dock we saw a small group of occupiers that had gathered to help load the wire onto my lifeboat. The wire was cut into 6 to 8-foot lengths, coiled with an overhand knot to make for easy handling, and piled on the dock.

Jack and I watched as they loaded the wire, but pretty soon I could see that there was more wire than seemed safe to take, as the gunnels were already within a few feet from the waterline. Just then I heard Jack behind me talking loudly to someone. I turned around and looked into the No.1 to see eight or nine Indians down in the hold, and they wouldn't come out. They wanted to get to shore in a bad way.

Then we noticed the others were still loading the remaining wire, and Jack looked at me and said, "It's time to go." He fired up the diesel and I undid the lines and pushed off, then jumped on board.

It didn't seem like the No.1 could pull this load, but Jack was cool, and went full-throttle as soon as we were out in the clear, chuckling at his tug's slow response to inch forward, fighting the current, the wind, and the loaded lifeboat. Besides us and the stowaways, we had a few more last-minute invited passengers. I remember asking him if he had any lifejackets and he held up two fingers and pointed down in the hold where two of the stowaways were now wearing lifejackets.

About half-way to Sausalito we noticed a Coast Guard vessel going incredibly fast with all but the keel out of the water! It wasn't your typical Coast Guard cutter, but an experimental jet-boat of some kind, and I never saw another one like it. This, of course, made us both a little nervous, worried that they might decide to check us out, but no, they had better things to do. We eventually made it back to Waldo Point, pulling in as close to the Ark parking lot as possible.

As soon as we got to shore all our passengers piled out and headed to the Bait Shop for food and drink, and since the truck that was supposed to be waiting to haul the copper to recycling had not yet arrived, to make a few phone calls. As we watch them walk away, Jack looks at me with his wry smile and kicks a few of the wire bundles overboard. So now the white man is once again ripping off the American Indian, and this time I'm guilty by association.

Over the next hour, while waiting for the truck, observing these guys put away a good amount of booze, and watching the waterline drop, as the tide was now going out, I noticed some wire poking above the surface just off the stern, visible to anyone looking hard enough. It was about that time the truck showed up and the wire was loaded. Luckily the extra wire went unnoticed and Jack went to get our money, while I felt relieved that we didn't start another Indian uprising.

POSTSCRIPT: *It was just a few weeks later, on June 11, 1971 that the remaining fifteen occupiers were forcibly removed by the U.S. government.*

Buck Knight giving me advice.

Syndrome

Now that Buck's back from Mexico
he threatens to kick everyone off the *Oakland.*
At night he drinks Bud and says,
    "What's happening daddy-o?"
In the morning he slams doors
and throws things in the Bay.
Last spring when the shop was turning into music
he sang with all his cowboy heart.
The Red Legs coached us and Jeff said,
    "Buck Bubbles and the Biodegradables are great!"
We all agreed.
But now he talks of leaving and law school,
everything pisses him off.
    "Remember Gibbons," and he twists his mouth,
    "The inability to concentrate on long range goals
    is a lower middle-class syndrome."

Postscript: I should point out that Jeff didn't really mean we were a great band, but liked Buck's voice and my name for the band, which was Buck Bubbles and the Biodegradable Booze Band. What Jeff really said was, "None of them were musicians, and Gibbons was the drummer."

Red Legs playing in Varda's yard after his ashes were tossed in the ocean.

The *Oakland* Shop

THE "LANDLORD" OF THE *OAKLAND* was Buck Knight, who rented the vessel from Don Arques, and sublet the two apartments and shop. Buck lived in the main pilothouse and rented the small wheelhouse to Maggie, who stored her art supplies there.

Jack the Fluke and his family lived in the middle apartment, adjacent to the shop, and the stern was occupied by Buck's hometown buddy, Jeremy.

There were five partners in the *Oakland* shop: Joe Tate; Jack Harshberger and Greg Baker, who had given themselves the genteel-sounding name, "Sausalito Shipwrights;" Jim Gibbons, a Milwaukee poet who was rigging out a clumsy but colorful 22-foot lifeboat conversion called the *Cowpie*; and a socially inept (even by waterfront standards) psychotic named Bob.

"Bob the Glob" was rigid all the way through, and had a steely-eyed glare in his eyes that called to mind "hatchet murderer." As Gibbons put it, "Bob had serious brain damage—and he didn't even drink!"

Bob hated the music and parties, and it wasn't long before he took action. One day I found the shop door locked, and a note taped to it: **"This is my shop, I want Joe Tate and his equipment out of here within 24-hours. If necessary, I will take legal action."**

The little turf was ended with a tense confrontation between Joe and Bob. People were drifting in to support Joe and the band, and "Bob the Glob" left the shop in defeat.

Baker and Harshberger eventually moved on, and the shop became the full- time practice and party room for the band, and social center for the neighborhood.

Gibbons remained, as he was having a good time, writing poetry about the waterfront scene and partying with the hippie chicks who often showed up when we were jamming.

Postscript: *"The Oakland Shop" was written by Jeff Costello in his memoir about the waterfront scene, Red Leg Boogie Blues, published in the Anderson Valley Advertiser, a weekly newspaper out of Boonville, California. Go to theava.com and click archives.*

Take Your Love and Shove it up Your Heart

Some say they love the way I hate you,
    but I still think I over-rate you
Your love is like a sinking vessel
    or tied down to a railroad trestle
And I've had plenty of it
    so take it back and shove it
Take your love and shove it up your heart!

Chorus: Take it, ram it, cram it, I don't care if you jam it
Just take your love and shove it up your heart!

Take your lies on a long vacation
    I'm fed up with your bad vibrations
I don't want love that says I must
    I don't eat pie that's solid crust
And I've had plenty of it
    so take it back and shove it
Take you love and shove it up your heart!

Chorus: Take it, ram it, cram it…etc.

You can eat your beans or you can sprout them
    You can trust your friends or you can doubt them
And one more thing before you go
    would make your exit way too slow
'Cuz I've had plenty of it
    so take it back and shove it
Take your love and shove it up your heart!

Chorus: Take it, ram it, cram it…etc.

One of Maggie's posters advertising the band's latest concert.

How I Got to Willits

I FIRST CAME TO WILLITS in late summer of 1971 because a fellow worker at the Tides Bookstore in Sausalito invited me up to see the property his girlfriend's family bought north of Willits.

Daniel Herreshoff was a grandson of a famous boat designer, naval architect, editor and author of books and magazines. The bottom line was Daniel had a trust fund set up so he didn't have to work, but that gets boring, so he got a part-time job at the Tides Bookstore.

Daniel was living with Stephanie and their little boy Max at her mom's house in San Francisco, spending much of the summers up on their Mendocino property, but he didn't seem to be a back-to-the-land kind of guy, just a cool, easy going dude with, according to a female admirer, "bedroom eyes."

Eventually Daniel and Stephanie split up and he moved to the windward side of Oahu with a new woman, but I haven't seen or heard from him since '86 when I was told by his new woman that he was in a 30-day detox center. He did like to drink, but I never saw him drunk, unless you count falling asleep during our conversations...*I know I'm loquacious, dude, but wake up!*

Speaking of drinking, one cool thing about the Tides location was that the *No Name Bar,* a favorite saloon for local celebs and boat people, happened to be right next door. I often stopped in for a beer after work.

One time I sat at the bar next to Spike Africa, a local legend who had been Sterling Hayden's first mate on the *Wanderer* in 1958 when Hayden defied a court order after a bitter divorce and sailed from Sausalito to Tahiti with his four kids. After Hayden returned he rented a pilot house on the *Berkeley*, a retired ferryboat docked in Sausalito, where many old boats ended up, and wrote his autobiography, *Wanderer*, which was published in 1963.

By the time I got there in '69 Hayden was living on a canal barge in Paris on the river Seine. His daughter, an attractive blond, lived in an old caboose on what was left of the original railroad tracks that ran north from the Sausalito waterfront all the way to Eureka.

What I remember about my conversation with Spike that evening was after mentioning, in an apologetic way, that my little sailboat was not sea-worthy and had no motor, he told me that is the best way to learn how to sail, especially around this Bay with the strong currents due to the relatively narrow Golden Gate. He added that if you learn how to sail in the San Francisco Bay you can sail anywhere in the world, and went on about "these so-called sailors in their plastic boats that turn on their engines whenever they get into trouble. What if their engines don't start?" And he chuckled at the thought.

That conversation really cheered me up and made me feel good about my sailing abilities, and it didn't hurt when Peter, the bartender, filled up my glass again, no charge, just because I was conversing with Spike Africa! I mean, who doesn't get excited around celebrities? Maybe other celebrities?

Speaking of celebrities, according to Joe Tate, a long-time local sailor and musician who still plays at the No Name every week, "I know that Marilyn Monroe and Burt Lancaster came in one night. While she sat in the corner near the stage, Burt got drunk and had to be ejected!" Joe also mentioned that the *No Name* now has a bust of Spike Africa.

Then there were the many young women who would come in the book-store, occasionally high on something or other, sometimes just high on life, and wanted to talk about it. Like the one who came in every week after *Monday Night Class*, her eyes sparkling with love for this guru Stephen Gaskin, which made me think either this guy was good, or she was loony. Probably both. He eventually got dozens of young followers together in several buses and caravanned back east, eventually starting a farming commune in Tennessee.

Some folks just came in for the coffee and to chat. We brewed coffee right next to the counter, which was convenient for friendly conversation. One woman looked at me and said, "Don't I know you?" It turned out to be someone I barely knew from high school back in Milwaukee who was now living in Point Richmond with the guy who used to date the girl I took to the Junior Prom, but I didn't know that yet.

She waited until I got off work and we went next door for a beer. We ended up back at her place, and though it did seem like she was living with someone, she didn't mention anyone and didn't seem concerned. She came in again a few days later, but then I didn't see her for a few weeks. I never got her number so one evening I thought I'd surprise her and stop by. He opened the door and looked at me like WTF are you doing here?!? I made something up that sounded really lame, and I heard her say from the other room, "Who is it, honey?"

After nearly a year as a part-time employee they offered me the job of paperback book buyer, to replace David, a nice English bloke who quit, eventually starting his own bookstore in Mill Valley. My first question was, do I have to work full-time, and the answer was, "Yes, six days a week."

From the moment I declined their offer things seemed to change. For one, my friend, Greg Baker, asked me to help him build a new boat, so I quit the Tides, only to be told a short time later that Greg couldn't get funding, so once again I was unemployed. Luckily, I qualified for unemployment because I quit one job for another job but that job didn't pan out. I got the minimum $26 a week, which was enough, with food stamps, to continue my humble lifestyle.

Sometime after that I drove up to Mendocino County with Daniel to check out the property. We stopped in Willits at an ice cream shop run by three elderly sisters, which later wound up in the Mendocino County Museum. The sisters dressed the same, wore the same matching red lipstick, as if they shared the same tube, and had their grey hair styled in matching perms. I remember one being friendlier than the other two, not that I could remember who was who. Next time you're in Willits, if you haven't done so before, check it out.

Andree wearing her see-through blouse.

Andree Conner's Hippie Van

OH, AND WHILE YOU'RE THERE, check out Andree Connor's hippie van, and the photo showing her rose tattoo where her left breast used to be. Yes, she had a mastectomy after diagnosed with breast cancer, and that photo of her rose tattoo, besides being on the cover of the local *New Settler* magazine displayed in the museum, was also in the national magazine, *New Woman*, which in today's speak, went viral, "giving way to acclaim and publication in books and magazines, nationally and internationally, thereby bringing much needed attention to the worldwide problem of breast cancer...she also appeared on the NBC Today Show in an interview about her choice."

That was from her obit. After a recurrence of the cancer in December of 2000, her wry sense of humor to the end, she planned her death by dressing in black and inviting a couple of close friends to be with her as she peacefully died in her home on January 13, 2001.

I mention Andree because I knew her in Sausalito. In fact, we dated for a short time in the late spring of '71. I first noticed her on Gene Lee's 30-foot lifeboat conversion that was tied up on the same finger dock at Gate 6 that I usually tied my little dory when I came ashore.

Gene Lee was a "chick magnet", always seeming to be the first choice of new female faces in the neighborhood, until he met Bonnie and they started doing heroin. The first time I ever shot heroin was with Gene in his van in the *Ark* parking lot. I should be embarrassed to admit that, but I was in my experiment-with-drugs phase, and what I learned was I really liked heroin so I better not take it again until I'm old and on my death bed.

Okay, I took it one more time with Hank the Hipster, but he called it a speedball, and I swear that was the last time! Anyhow, I'd like to think that Andree went out high on heroin. Modern medicine doesn't get much better than that.

The first time I met Andree was at a neighborhood party. She had a cute face surrounded by a light brown afro, her braless breasts peeking seductively through her loose fitting top, everything else hidden by a maxi skirt. Anyhow, I ended up back on her boat, but not for the night, which I could live with, though I did want to stay, for a few reasons. I mean, I'd had a bit too much to smoke and drink, and my boat had recently blown onto the rocks at Strawberry Point during the last southerly storm at high tide. So, I had to wait about two weeks for the tide to get high enough to pull it off the rocks.

Meanwhile, to get home wasn't that easy. I'd have to row across the bay to Strawberry Point, negotiate the rocks and make sure my dory was safe from getting banged up by any rogue waves in the middle of the night. I guess the other reason I didn't want to go home that night was she made me real horny.

The next morning I wrote a poem for Andree and gave it to her that evening. She seemed more surprised than impressed, but my plan worked and she let me stay the night. We hung out for a few weeks, long enough for me to get my boat off the rocks and take her sailing.

I have a photo of her sitting on my cabin holding her knees up under her maxi skirt, her smile almost visible through her fuzzy hairdo. There wasn't much wind so we floated with the out-going tide past the dry docks (now gone), and as usual the wind picked up about the time the Golden Gate Bridge was fully visible. But the tide was changing so we sailed in a big circle and headed back.

No, we didn't really become a couple, I mean, it was the era of free love and hippie chicks were like free candy to a sugar junky, which made it more difficult to hang with one woman for very long. And then one day she was gone. I think she bought Gene Lee's van and hit the road, and I must say, the one in the Willits museum sure looks like it.

Anyhow, a week later there was a feature article written by her in the *Sunday Chronicle's California Living Magazine* about the Gates, with photos. She did not even tell me she was a writer, and I never saw her again. Well, not in person, but about twenty years later I was listening to a KMFB radio show out of Fort Brag called "On the Record," with host Ed Kowas, and heard her voice. At first, I didn't really think it was her, but it was, and I found out she and Ed were a couple.

WHEN TO BE AFRAID OF BEARS

Daniel and I made it up to their property and he showed me around. There were no structures, but I noticed a decent size pile of new dimensional redwood. He told me the story of how it got there. A neighbor noticed a few railroad cars, including one flat car full of redwood lumber, left down by Outlet Creek just east of Highway 101. It sat there for days, so one weekend Daniel came up and helped his neighbor "remove it." I asked what he was going to build with it, which prompted him to say, "You're welcome to come up and build something with it."

The thought of getting away from the waterfront for the winter really appealed to me, and to build a small structure in the wilderness was also something I suddenly wanted to do. About that time, I met Yvonne and she liked the idea too, so we decided to go for it. I sold my boat to Jeremy for $500, which I figured with my meager unemployment, food stamps from Marin, and bulk food from Mendocino, was enough to make it through the winter.

This Shimmins Ridge property was not that accessible, being three miles up a winding dirt road from the highway, and 15 miles from Willits. Obviously there was no electricity, but there was a spring half-way up to the ridge where the owners got their gravity-feed water to the campsite, and a small wood burning cook stove they intended to put in the building they planned to build, but after three summers of just camping out on weekends and spending those hot afternoons at Cherry Creek, the local swimming hole, they again went back to San Francisco for the winter months, giving me the chance to see what I could build with the pile of redwood they scored.

I decided to build a 12 X 12-foot structure up on the side of the hill, just below the spring, which gave us a better view, a bit more winter sun, and still gravity flow for running water. The first thing I had to do was buy some building materials, a few tools, and other needed supplies. The fact that Yvonne was willing to share this adventure with me really helped, I mean, I don't think I would have done it alone.

I met Yvonne through Gil Stewart, a local street mechanic who told me he just met a woman whose VW bus broke down up on Donner Pass in the Sierras, and was looking for someone to tow it back to the Bay Area so he could work on it. Knowing that I had a pick-up, he asked if I wanted to meet her.

Everyone knows the story of the Donner Party that got snowbound up there and survived through the winter of 1846-47 eating the more tasty parts of their dead friends and neighbors. It's no surprise that the youngest and oldest died first, or that the young ones tasted a lot better, although I'm just speculating. Back then I guess they called that surviving, but today they call it cannibalism. 48 of 87 were eventually rescued, and what a story they had to tell their grandchildren, if there were any left.

I arranged to meet her the next day and agreed to tow her bus back to Mill Valley for $20, but we got a late start, and when we finally arrived at the Donner Lake campsite, where her bus sat with its puny 4-cylinder, 40 horsepower engine blown, it was too late in the day to head down the mountain, so we sat around the campfire and got to know each other better.

We seemed to hit it off, and near the end of the evening she asked me if I was afraid of bears. My first reaction was no, before really thinking it through. I mean, we were up in a mountain wilderness where marauding bears love nothing better than to ransack campsites for human food. When she said goodnight, I watched her get into her cozy VW bus, wondering what the hell was I thinking! I should have said yes, and then she may have invited me to join her.

I laid there by the dying campfire for a few more minutes, staring up at the stars, wondering what I would do if a bear did show up? Would I be safer here on the ground in my sleeping bag or in the back of my open-bed pick-up truck? I decided the safest spot would be in her completely protected cozy camper.

So, I gently knocked on the door and said, "Yvonne, I've decided that I'm afraid of bears, too." She let me in and we lived together for ten years, had two boys, and looking back I think that was one of the best decisions I ever made.

Another Dead Dog 1975

WILL THE PERSON WHO SHOT my dog down by Outlet Creek read this? I hate not knowing why she was shot. Was her friendly tail-wagging threatening you? Was it a mercy killing? Target practice? Any words about the incident would be nice, but I don't expect to hear from you.

She was a small tan, wire-haired terrier who answered to the name of Scrambler, but any name from a friendly voice would do. She was about as dangerous as a pack of newts or a herd of bunny rabbits.

On Tuesday, March 4, driving north out of Willits, we picked up a young hitch-hiker going to Cherry Creek. We took him the extra few miles, and when we mentioned our dog was missing he told us about a neighbor who shoots any dogs trespassing on his property. It seemed unlikely that they would go that far. They include Yvonne's yellow lab, Tala, Scrambler's partner in crime. They would sometimes disappear for an hour or so, but they always came back, so we never worried about them.

We dropped off the hitch-hiker and coming back on Covelo Road, about two miles east of Highway 101, we saw a few vultures circling what looked like a carcass on the water's edge. Yvonne, the emotional part of the family, cried out "Scrambler!"

I replied, matter-of-factly, "It's not Scrambler!" At the same time braking, checking the rear- view mirror, and turning around to go back.

Yvonne didn't want to go look, so I slid down the steep bank and walked toward the carcass, shooing the stubborn turkey vultures away, and there she was, her entrails half out on the dry gravel, her eyes pecked out, and a hole the size of a Kennedy half-dollar in her rib cage.

I was both numb and relieved. She had been gone ten days. Tala and I had searched the hills in vain. I had heard there were a "pack of wild dogs" roaming these woods, but I don't think she was abducted or joined the pack and went feral. Maybe the person who started that rumor confused "wild dogs" with the coyotes we heard howling in the evenings.

One theory of Yvonne's was she was kicked in the head by the feisty pony that roams these hills and chases dogs. We just didn't understand why she didn't come home. She was no sheep or chicken killer. She ate Chuck Wagon garnished with table scraps. We had a crotchety old hen that chased her once in a while, but she never hankered for revenge.

She was born on a houseboat in Gate 5, Sausalito, the runt and only female of the litter. Toothless Tom named her because she always scrambled over her bigger brothers, usually ending up in the bilge. The day Tom put her in my hands, Pam Massie was there declaring that a dog was just what a happy bachelor needed.

I took her everywhere I went, except Mexico that June. Jeremy gladly took care of her, as he stayed on my boat while I was gone. When I returned, she surprised both of us by dancing and prancing and carrying on like she was all happy to see me, so I continued taking her sailing and riding shotgun in my '57 Ford pick-up, never feeling the least bit embarrassed for actually feeling attached to something so small and furry and useless.

A month or so later we met Yvonne and Tala, a perfect fit, so I sold my boat to Jeremy and we came up here to the mountains. This area seemed really wild in 1971. I built a modest, far-from-code cabin and we huddled around the woodstove at night listening to the dogs talk to the coyotes.

When spring finally came, so did Joan and Stephanie, the mom and daughter who owned the property. They had been coming up in the summer for a few years, but never built anything, so it was always a camping trip. They were impressed with my efforts, and couldn't wait to move in.

That was fine with me and Yvonne, because my sister Sherry said we could stay on the family farm. The family farm was located in northern Wisconsin, and included a small lake that my Uncle Freddie used to take me fishing on. I sometimes tell people I grew up on a farm, but that's an embellishment, as I actually spent the school year in the Milwaukee suburbs, only going up to the farm in the summer and some holidays. But there was something about my memories of the farm that drew me to the woods of Mendocino County.

The reason I wanted to go back to Wisconsin was because Sherry's seven-year-son, Ian, had recently been diagnosed with leukemia (lympho-sarcome), and I really wanted to see him. Erv and Sherry also had twins, Neil and Kira. Kira was healthy, but Neil was born with a cleft palate, so between work, doctor appointments, and other family obligations they were plenty busy, and I wanted to help out.

When I first got the news, I wanted to send something, so I made a book I named *Uncle Jim, Mountain Man*. I was never really an artist, but drew this cartoonish story about our first winter in the mountains, and when I was done Yvonne was surprised how good it was, which made me feel more confident, so I sent it.

By the time we got back to Wisconsin, Ian had died (March 26, 1972), and on the first evening visiting Sherry and Erv I was curious if Ian got the book I sent. When I asked Sherry, she said, "Yes, he loved it." This prompted me to ask if I could look at it. She said Ian was holding it close to his chest when he died, so they buried it with him.

The other topic was the family farm, but they had decided to sell it, so we went looking for a place on the east side of Milwaukee. I looked up a few old friends and luckily my old high school buddy Dennis Papp had a rental on the Milwaukee River with a small unit in the back for just $50 a month, and they didn't mind the dogs. In fact, Dennis and Ramona had a six-year-old daughter, Tina, who was really fond of Scrambler, a dog her size. One day, skipping along beside me as we walked the dogs, she asked, "Gibbons, why is Scrambler's tongue so small?"

For the first time, I realized she did have a small tongue, even for her size, but it felt like soft velvet when she eased it down between my toes after a hard day moving cow hides from the railroad cars to the ships down at the Port of Milwaukee.

One time, Scrambler disappeared for two days. I was sitting on our front steps, feeling kind of low, when she comes running up all excited, wagging her tail like crazy, and the stranger says, "Don't worry, she won't bite."

"I know, because she's my dog! I said, a bit too unfriendly. He didn't believe me at first, but then Yvonne comes outside all happy and convincing, and he says, apologetically, "She followed me home and I thought…"

Maybe she decided to follow someone else again and caught the bullet coming home? Getting hit by a car would have been easier to take, but the good news is it's over. I dug a shallow grave under a river ash and dragged her into the hole. I wanted to keep part of her. Her tail, tongue, a paw for good luck…does that sound sick? It just seemed like such a waste to bury her out of sight. I partly understood why Roy Rogers had Trigger and Bullet stuffed. Anyhow, I covered her with sand and dirt, rolled a big rock on top. And would have written, if I had something to write with:

UNDER THIS ROCK LIES SCRAMBLER
ANOTHER DEAD DOG
1971 -- 1975

Do Yvonne and I look happy enough with our new baby?

Milwaukee Has Caught Me

I stare at the TV and pick at my nose
I sit in the barrooms until the doors close

Oh, Milwaukee has caught me, that city of beer
And everyone asks me, "What you doing back here?"

I left here one winter, my thumb pointed west
And made it to Waldo, the place I like best

But the magnet was stronger, it pulled and it tugged
Must be brain damage, at best I've been drugged!

Oh, I'll always remember my friends on the Bay
How we laughed and got fucked up at least once a day

But nostalgia aside I could hardly have known
Brain damage is fun 'til you're left all alone.

I WROTE THE ABOVE LYRICS to the tune of *Wildwood Flower,* an old country hit by the Carter Family, which included of course, June Carter, who married Johnny Cash.

Yvonne's dad, Elvin Jolley, was into old country music, especially Hank Williams and Jimmie Rodgers, the *Blue Yodeler.* He showed me a few chords on his old Harmony f-hole guitar, then before we left for Wisconsin that spring of '72, he gave me the guitar and a few of his old song books.

When we got back to Milwaukee I would practice the main three chords that many of those songs used, and sometimes just for fun, make up new lyrics to the songs. My main problem was I didn't like my voice, and although creating new lyrics seemed to help me practice, it wasn't enough to keep plugging away, and just like the poetry scene I got tired of, I soon lost interest in playing the guitar.

Once we got settled into our little Milwaukee rental, we had two problems. Yvonne's little 36-hp VW engine blew a cylinder, and we were broke. I told her since I had paid for everything since we'd been together (only about nine months), it was her turn to get a job. She agreed, but said if she was going to get a job she wanted to do something that paid more than minimum wage, so she got a job as a go-go dancer at a bar on the south side.

Three nights a week she would have to take the bus to this popular southside bar, until I finally got the VW engine replaced, and decided to surprise her by picking her up at work. I remember showing up about midnight, entering this packed bar, and seeing her up on this platform shaking her booty. I was somewhat surprised how sexy she looked in her butt thong and bare breasts, though she had pasties over her nipples, as Milwaukee didn't allow too topless go-go dancers.

Seeing all the guys clapping and staring at her made me feel both proud and embarrassed, but since I didn't know anyone, it was our little secret. I don't recall how much she made, or maybe I never asked, but she paid for the new engine, food, and the next month's rent, so life was good and I didn't complain.

In the evenings when she was working I would often stop over at Ed and Vickie's third floor apartment to drink beer and swap stories. They came out to visit me in Sausalito in 1970, and I took them sailing on the *Cowpie,* so they were familiar with the waterfront scene.

Ed had printed my book of poems, *Prime the Pump,* on his letterpress in 1970, and my new manuscript, to be named *Mud Grudge,* was all ready to go. Problem was he didn't want to use Maggie Siegfried's drawings, but I really liked them, from Bad Dog walking in the mud, to Ebbie reading a book, to Andree wearing her seductive see-through blouse. The likeness was always amazing, and she did each drawing for a specific poem.

Ed was busier than ever publishing many other poets, and became quite in demand, probably because he didn't charge anyone. If he decided to publish your book, no charge. In fact, he was insulted if you offered him money, as I learned in 1985, thirteen years after I gave him my manuscript. Thinking that some money would prod him into finally getting it done, I sent him a $500 check, but he never cashed it.

The bottom line was he never did print my second book, and to this day (July 3, 2017) it's been forty-seven years and still no second book. I've had a few opportunities, but made some bad decisions, or maybe I have what my old waterfront friend Jeff called, "The built-in failure factor."

Here's one example. Back on the waterfront in 1971, a friend told me a woman was publishing a book of photos of the many colorful Sausalito houseboats, to be called *Water Squaters*. She had read my book and wondered if I had more waterfront poems for her book. I told him I did, but my friend back in Milwaukee already had my manuscript and would be publishing it real soon. Her book came out and I could see that my poems would have fit really well. That's a regret to measure on my *Regret-O-Meter!*

Ed was a carpet layer in the daytime, and I sometimes worked with him when he had bigger jobs. Not much fun to crawl around on your hands and knees, but it wasn't steady work, and not only did I feel good about helping him out now and then, but made a little spending money so I wouldn't be dependent on Yvonne.

One night over at Ed's I was telling him that Yvonne wanted me to get a job. I told him, "She's been nagging me on a regular nine-to-five, forty hour-a-week schedule."

He jumped up and said, "Write that down." He gave me a pen and some paper, and within a week he had printed a slew of postcards.

Plus Overtime
I think she wants me
to get a job.
She's been nagging on a regular
9 to 5, 40 hour a week
schedule.

Then one Friday night I stopped over and met their babysitter, Jill, a cute 18-year-old recent high school grad who wanted to know all about San Francisco and Sausalito. Since Ed and Vickie were out, and six-year old Morgan was in bed, I told her a few tales of my days sailing around the Bay and down the Coast to Mexico. We seemed to hit it off, so I invited her to stop over Saturday night and I'd show her some photos I had of the Bay Area.

Later, when I got home, Yvonne was already there, puking in the toilet. She said she was pregnant and quit her job. Wow! I was going to be a dad! The next night I stopped over to Ed and Vickie's to tell them the good news. So much was going through my brain I forgot that I had invited Jill over to the house, so while I'm visiting Ed and Vickie, Yvonne is home alone and hears a knock on the door.

At some point during my visit I suddenly remembered, tried to call Jill from Ed's, but no answer, so I left hurriedly, but when I got home, Yvonne sneered, "Your friend Jill was here earlier," and went on to describe the sexy, low-cut top she was wearing.

Ouch.

ELI'S BIRTH 1973

Now that I was going to be a dad, it was time for me to get a real job, so I went to *Man Power* to see what they had. I ended up working full time at the *Manufacturing Box Company* on the clean-up shift, from 3:15 to 11:45.

Just me and a grumpy old German guy who taught me the proper way to sweep the floor and scrape the dried glue off the machines. I also disposed of the glue and cardboard trash in a dumpster, with a lever that moved a steel top shut, so the trash can be pressed tightly before being pushed out.

Grumpy German Guy warned me not to stick my hand back in the machine once I activate the lever or "You could lose an arm." A few weeks after I quit, I heard the guy who replaced me did just that, trying to push down some cardboard after activating the lever, and somehow got his right arm caught. It was cut off just below his elbow.

I worked there all winter until spring when a friend said they were hiring at the Port of Milwaukee. In April I became a Longshoreman, making over $5 per hour, two dollars more than the Box company paid, and three dollars more than minimum wage. Unions were strong back in those days, but sadly, those days are gone.

Yvonne was expecting in late May or early June, and would deliver in the hospital with the help of two nurse midwives. I was there watching the baby crown when one of the midwives came over and told me I better sit down, and helped me to a chair.

Her concerned look reminded me that I was pale and starting to swoon, but I was so mesmerized by Eli's crowning head.

Eli Robert Gibbons was a healthy, 7-pound, 2-ounce boy with dark curly hair like his mom. We decided on Eli Robert because her dad's name was Elvin (I dropped the v and the n), and my dad was Robert.

More newly married couples were combining their last names with a hyphen, which would make us Jolley-Gibbons. What would be a good name for our son if his last name was Jolley-Gibbons?

I decided Midas, as in King Midas, would be a cool first name. And Welby, as in the popular TV show, *Marcus Welby, M.D.* would give him the perfect name for keeping a stiff upper lip when times were tough.

Midas Welby Jolley-Gibbons. I didn't push it because we never got married, and I didn't want to. I mean, it was the seventies, and people were living together without bothering to tie the knot. I'd already been married and divorced by the time I was twenty-five. Who needs the hassle?It was tough quitting my job at the Port of Milwaukee in October '73, just one month before being laid off and getting unemployment all winter, but decided we didn't want to spend another winter in Milwaukee. So once again I was heading west, but this time with Yvonne and 4-month-old Eli.

We decided to head southwest to San Diego where Yvonne grew up and her family still lived. I naively thought I could get a job at the Port of San Diego, but I guess my resume didn't quite do the trick, so after spending Thanksgiving with her family, I left her and Eli at her parent's place for a few weeks and drove up to Sausalito to see what was going on at the Gates.

I was happy to be back to see old friends, and decided I would rather live on a houseboat in Sausalito than in San Diego, and it just so happened that Joe Tate had a 35-foot *Captain's Gig* he was willing to rent to us. This was a narrow 35-foot motor boat used to ferry naval officers back and forth from ships anchored offshore during World War II

It was tied up to a sunken WW II sub-chaser, that was tied up to the *Oakland*, the sunken potato boat I stayed on when I first came out from Milwaukee in the spring of '69. This was the same shop I shared with Greg Baker and Bill Becker, who were both rebuilding sailboats, and helped me with mine.

Becker sailed to Hawaii, Greg moved onto his boat, I met Yvonne and took her up to Mendocino, where I built a small cabin in the woods north of Willits. The shop was soon taken over by Joe Tate and all his musical followers.

I'd been away from the waterfront for over two years, and during that time The *Red Legs* had really improved, and getting more out of town gigs. The *Red Legs* were the local rock and roll band led by Joe Tate, the singer and rhythm guitar player. Maggie was the "chick singer" and the artist who made the posters (and the drawings in this book). Jeff was lead guitar, Kim played bass, and Joey Crunch was on drums. They all lived on the waterfront, which made it easier to have spontaneous jam sessions, and those jam sessions took place in the *Oakland* shop.

I had taken the *Red Legs* to a few gigs before I left Waldo, because I was the only one with a pick-up truck. Now that I'm back, Joe tells me they have a gig up in northern Mendocino County in a little bar called *Choo Choo Mama's*.

Since the VW bus could carry both passengers and drum equipment, I agreed to take them. But the band had a few problems. One was that Joey had become a heroin addict, sometimes passing out in the middle of a gig, or at least he did at *Choo Choo Mama's* the night my brief musical career came to an end.

Tate thought that Joey had taught me some basics and that I could keep a beat, so with Joey passed out in the back room, he told me to sit in for the second set. The truth was although I wanted to learn the drums, and Joey was going to teach me the basics, he always seemed too busy scoring some dope and sharing it with Maria, his sweetie.

So, I sat down and right away both Joe Tate and Jeff looked at me like, "Dude, can't you keep a fucking beat?!?" It was hopeless, and finally Tate asked if there were any drummers in the audience. Sure enough, a guy came up and took my place, to everyone's relief, and I melted into the crowd.

My next challenge was returning to San Diego and convincing Yvonne to live with me and Eli on the waterfront in a World War II vessel without electricity or bathroom amenities.

OUT THE WINDOW FE 4, 1974

Yvonne was willing to return to Gate 6 with me and live on Joe Tate's 35-foot Captain's Gig, but there was one thing I neglected to tell her. Our new rental was tied up to the stern of a sunken sub-chaser, and the community crapper was on the bow.

When she found out, I told her what Becker told me when I first arrived, the tide comes in and goes out twice a day, which makes it self-flushing. The unwritten rule was don't take a dump at low tide, and if you can, make sure the tide is going out.

Our new floating home was very narrow, only eight feet across, which made me wonder how they ever got the big wood cook stove that took up half of the kitchen space, inside in the first place. The other question I never asked was why was the boat named the *Tree Frog?* I mean, there wasn't a tree within sight.

The bed was in what used to be the pilot house, and was raised 4-feet above the floor, making it even with the bottom of the tall, wrap-around windows, giving us the same 180-degree view while in bed that the helmsman had back in the day.

One of the four large windows on the starboard side opened outward, which was handy for a little sea breeze, but could be scary if you had an energetic eight-month-old crawling around the bed. I always made sure it was latched before I brought him into bed with us, but for some reason it wasn't secure that morning he was fussing in his crib.

I brought him into bed with us, as he liked to look out the windows, point at seagulls or the egrets who wade for food at low tide. The boat was sitting on the mud, but there was still a few feet of water out there.

While Yvonne and I were taking our last morning hug, the window suddenly opened and he was gone. We didn't see him fall out, but my body reacted like a spring, as I jumped out the window and looked down to see him going under water. Time seemed to slow down as I fell feet first into the shallow water and picked him up in one fell swoop, just as he was taking a breath.

He was wet, with fresh mud smeared on his head, but hadn't swallowed any water, so while I'm holding him up like a trophy, I see Yvonne's smile of relief and hand him up to her.

The rickety floating walkways were scary for anyone, especially kids who were just learning to walk, and this was another reason Yvonne wanted to leave the waterfront.

Problem was I had just been hired by my old friend Roy Cano to help him do a routine bottom job that turned into a more serious repair job, replacing pieces of the old rotten wooden hull, and then calking and painting. The job was a few weeks longer than we expected, but the money was needed, and Roy was a fun guy to work and hang out with.

The good news was that Yvonne had a new friend, Pam, who also had a boy about Eli's age, named Dory, and they would hang out together in a small area behind the *Ark*, which had become a makeshift playground.

Dory's dad was Goldie, a local fisherman who was a good generation older than Pam, but seemed mellow, which may have had something to do with his heroin addiction. He eventually cleaned up, but not before the tragic day Pam left him to watch Dory while she went to the store. Somehow Dory fell off the pier and was found floating face down between the finger dock and their boat.

This was all Yvonne could handle, and wanted to get Eli away from the waterfront ASAP! We found a geodesic dome for rent up on Shimmins Ridge, about twelve miles north of Willits. She waited there with Eli while I finished my job with Roy, and then I joined her.

The Discovery

I learned something about myself tonight
My name: GIBBONS
I was playing with it rather harmlessly
When it broke between the B's
But like a child I was unsatisfied
So I fooled with each part
Not unlike one mesmerized by Post Alphabits
When suddenly like Clark Kent it changed
Each part backwards: BIG SNOB.
You can imagine the shock of such a discovery
And at my age.

Me in family photo, clean shaven, but without shoes.
Sitting from left to right: Jeff Firzlaff, Neal Zaporski,
Bob Gibbons, Me, Eli, and Renee Zaporski.
Behind us from left to right: Kathy Firzlaff,
Sherry Zaporski, Kira Zaporski, and Vickie Firzlaff.

He's Not Heavy, Father

AFTER DIGGING OUT OF THE Big Snow of February, 1975, I checked in at the Mendocino County unemployment office in Ukiah because my six months of $31 a week had run out. I was asked about my last job, and told them I was repairing wooden boats in Sausalito, but willing to take any carpentry or labor job. Within a few weeks I was sent to Laytonville for an interview for a CETA job.

CETA (Comprehensive Employment and Training Act) was a public works relief program that Nixon signed into law in December of '73, not long before he left office in disgrace because of the Watergate Scandal. Like Roosevelt's CCC (Civilian Conservation Corps) my dad worked on in the 30s, it was established to train workers and provide them with jobs in the public service. The main difference was the CCC was only for unmarried men 18-25 who were from needy families, but let my dad tell it from an interview my niece Renee did in 1988 for a high school history project regarding someone who experienced the Great Depression.

"I went in 1933 when I got out of high school. They sent me to Lost Corners, Arkansas to build fire trails up in the Ozark Mountains. I was there for 15 months. I got $30 a month to start, $5 for me and they sent $25 to my mother to help with my two younger sisters. It was just like an army camp, in fact, we wore old clothes that were from World War I. The War had only been over for 14 years by that time. Anyhow, we were fed well and treated decent and it was a good experience."

On the morning I was to report for my interview I woke up early, determined to get there on time, which I did, but it was a struggle. It was still dark when I went downstairs to make some coffee, and although I lit a kerosene lamp for some light, I didn't see a clean cup so I reached into the dark sink and AAHHH! It felt like a sliver of glass went into my finger. I quickly grabbed a flashlight and pointed down to see a scorpion waving his tail at me, with a taunting *you-want-another-piece-of-me?* attitude.

I didn't see anything in my forefinger, but it stung like hell! I had heard their stingers were poisonous, and wondered what the effects would be, as I continued to get ready to leave, still determined to get to the Laytonville yard by 7:30.

When I arrived, I walked in holding my painful, still throbbing finger and met Walt, the yard boss. I told him what happened and he seemed impressed that I still made it on time, but told me these northern scorpions are not poisonous like the ones down south, which I was tending to believe anyhow, since it had already been over an hour and I had no other symptoms. I was to report to work the following Monday to join a crew of nine other newly-hired locals to build a path along Branscomb Road from just east of the yard to town, less than two miles.

Locals on this Laytonville crew were made up mostly of back-to-the-land guys from either Spyrock Road or Bell Springs Road, though one guy came all the way down from Piercy. Chas, our crew leader, was the only one from Willits. When we moved from Covelo Road to Sherwood Road that Summer I would drive the six miles to town and meet Chas, then he'd drive us the 24 miles to the Laytonville yard, chatting all the way. Chas had a good sense of humor, an attractive wife, two young girls, and a nice house in the Little Lake Valley. But he complained about the wife and her live-in father, so it didn't surprise me when they split up and he eventually moved back to Utah.

Back to my dad's 1930s: **"I started high school in 1930, when the depression really started, and graduated in '34. Avoca, Iowa was a small town and we had a class of only 34 people. It was a pretty rough time, for example, farmers were getting 10 to 12 cents a bushel for** corn, and you could buy a big chicken for a quarter. In fact, we didn't have meat very often…mostly on Sunday. My mother's small home was heated by a pot-bellied stove and we had a wood burning cook stove. We were in a small town, like I said, but we had outdoor plumbing. In that part of town there weren't many people who had sewage. It was a rough go, but everybody was in the same boat, so you never felt poor."

In contrast to the limited opportunities my dad had in the 30s depression era, the 70s offered plenty of opportunities, at least for young healthy white guys like me. Yet, I was restless and bored, preferring the hippie lifestyle over full-time employment, and not really knowing what I wanted, but knowing dam well what I didn't want. I guess you could say I "tuned in, turned on, and dropped out." And to me that also meant "going off the grid." Life is so different without being able to just flick a switch to turn on the lights or the heater. I figure I've spent about half my life off the grid.

I walked away from some pretty good jobs in my life, too. Jobs my dad would have been happy to get. For example, I got a job at the Sausalito Post Office soon after taking the multiple-choice test because I scored a 96 and they hired according to test scores. The reason I did so well on the test was because at that point I had spent most of my life in school taking tests. Then just two weeks before I was to get tenure, I was fired because I wouldn't shave my beard and cut my hair, and according to my termination letter, they didn't like the clothes I wore. But like the full-time jobs I'd lost before, I felt relieved. I hated working full-time, unless it was just half the year, with unemployment the other half.

But perhaps I should reveal the real reason I was fired. I was working the 2 am to 10 am shift with just one other guy. At one point, I had to go into the boss's office for something and saw a roll of his name tags: Anthony L. Medeiros. I tore one off and just for fun wondered if it would stick in the men's bathroom urinal. It did. Sometime after 6 AM when other employees started punching in I heard laughter coming from the men's room. I went in and saw that it was still just where I put it. I peed on it one more time and emerged smiling like the others, except unlike the others I knew for sure who did it. Soon I was called into the boss's office and told to shave my beard and cut my shoulder length hair before returning to work the next day. The urinal prank was not mentioned.

For years after that my dad would say, "Jim, you should have kept that job at the post office." No, I never told him I was fired, and never regretted losing that job, or any job, though I did really like working at the Tides Bookstore in downtown Sausalito because it was part-time and you never knew who would come in next.

Richard Brautigan, one of my favorite poets at the time, used to come in every so often just to see how his books were selling. Once Professor Irwin Corey, the comedian I had seen on the Johnny Carson *Tonight Show*, walked in, looked at me and I loudly welcomed him, "Professor?!" His response was, "This ain't no bar!" And turned around and left. I stood there staring at the door, wishing I had kept quiet. The *No Name Bar* was next door, which made his reaction to me even funnier.

Another one of my favorite poets, Gary Snyder, came in and after perusing the poetry section came over to the register with several books, including my book, which happened to be displayed in the window at the time. This prompted me to introduce myself, telling him what a fan I was, and wondered what made him choose it. He smiled while opening it to the introductory quote of his, "One does not need universities and libraries, one need be alive to what is about."

Then I invited him to go sailing with me the next day, but he declined. Said he was living in the Sierra foothills just outside of Nevada City, and had a small crew helping him build a house without using any power tools. He invited me to stop by if I was ever in the neighborhood, which I actually did four years later while on a mission with a friend to get fir poles for spars, booms, and masts.

A waterfront buddy named Chris had a Dodge flat-bed truck with a long bed and asked me to go with him up to North San Juan in the Sierra's to get some fir poles, saying the straight ones grow on the north slope, and mentioned that Gary Snyder lived up where we were going. I told him about the time Gary came into the *Tides Bookstore* and invited me to stop in if I was ever in the neighborhood.

Chris was up for it, so a few days later on our way up the north slope of this mountain road we saw a big parking lot in the middle of nowhere, with a sign that read OFFICE.

"Wow, Snyder sure has gotten commercial," I said, before realizing it was the *Ananda Retreat*, a hippie commune right next door to Snyder's place. So, we parked and walked down this quarter-mile long path to this yard surrounded by Japanese inspired architecture. A group of people were looking at us. First, I recognized Allen Ginsberg, then saw Snyder with a serious look on his face. As they approached I said to Gary, "You probably don't recognize me." He agreed and I continued, telling him about the time he stopped in the *Tides Bookstore*, and then he smiled, slowly moving his head up and down, as he seemed to recollect that day four years earlier.

Then I said to Ginsberg, "Hi Allen, you probably don't recognize me," and told him about the time I met him in Milwaukee at Barbara Gibson's place. He remembered and said how much he liked Barbara's latest book of poetry, *This Woman*. Gary agreed, touting it as the best book of poetry by a woman in years, before politely excusing himself and asking Allen to show us around.

At one point, we were invited into Gary's "meditation room," but as I attempted to walk through the door, Allen said, "Shoes, you must take off your shoes." We had boots on and didn't want to bother, and then declined his invitation to walk down the hill to see his place. We had to get going and thanked him, said hello, goodbye to Gary and his beautiful Japanese wife, and split.

In retrospect, I often feel bad about my dad's only surviving son being such a hippie. I mean, I never thought of myself as a hippie, but old photos don't lie. Like the summer of '76 when I brought Eli back to Milwaukee during my barefoot phase. I had met Carl Carlson working on that CETA job and he turned me on to Tai Chi, which I liked doing barefoot. It felt so good I eschewed shoes for months—unbelievable! I even boarded the plane back to Milwaukee without shoes on, no problem. There's a family portrait of all of us, me sitting in the front row, barefoot. The photo also reminds me that my mother was more upset about my full beard, so I shaved it off, which made her so pleased…until a week later when she mentioned it was growing back and I said, "Mom, I shaved for you, but I never said I was going to shave again!"

Funny thing, Dad had a tough life, but I never heard him complain, whereas I shunned the good life and complained all the time—and still do! When he was nine or ten his dad was run over by a milk wagon and his mom couldn't feed the four of them on the $25-a-month widow's pension, so he was sent to *Boy's Town*. Back to Renee's interview with Grandpa.

"Before I started high school—you've probably heard of Father Flanagan's *Boy's Town* in Omaha. My mother was living in Omaha at the time and one aunt took one of my sisters, another went into a home, and my mother sent me to *Boy's Town*. I was there from the time I was 11 to 13. Father Flanagan's didn't start until about 1917, so when I was there in '26 he was the guiding light. They had a big farm outside of Omaha where we milked cows and grew our own food. I was there recently and I would never have recognized it."

His mention of being there "recently" was in 1983 when my son Eli was ten and qualified to run the National Junior Olympics Cross Country Championships, which were held that year at *Boy's Town*. The day after Eli qualified I called my Dad and told him, so he flew down from Milwaukee to meet us there. I remember him saying he would have never recognized it, except for that statue of the two boys, one carrying the other one, saying, "He's not heavy Father, he's my brother."

Let's wrap this up with a few more quotes:

"The Rock Island Railroad wasn't too far from us, and they used the coal stored there for the engines to go to the adjoining towns off the main line, and that's where we got our coal for heat. Usually we did are "shopping" in the dark, at night, if you know what I mean. But that wasn't unusual either. The sheriff turned his back. He didn't see anything and didn't want to, and even the railroad detectives didn't care much either.

There were all kinds of ideas being tossed around during those times because of poverty, but I never got too carried away with so-called socialism. There are certain things that did develop out of it, such as social security and Medicare for the elderly…well, the war was on the horizon, you could see it. There was a real nut in that Hitler. Anyway, in about 1940 business started picking up fast because of military work, and a lot of kids were going into the service…you could see that there was going to be problems, but no one ever dreamed of Pearl Harbor. Hitler was obvious, but the Japanese? I think to most people, except maybe scholars, that was a real shock."

An old photo of Bob and Ida Gibbons. circa ~1937.

My granddaughter Makayla at beer o'clock.

I'd Rather Have a Bottle in Front of Me

I'VE BEEN HAVING A BEER or two in the evening before dinner ever since my dad offered me that first Pabst Blue Ribbon when I was just 16-years-old. He believed that responsible drinking started at home and ended down at the local tavern at closing time.

No, I'm kidding. Seriously though, my parents and their friends were social drinkers. To their credit, I don't recall any physical or verbal abuse, or out-of-control drunkenness among the lot—and we're talking Irish and German ancestry here. I like to tell people I'm half German and half Irish--a disciplined drunk.

My dad was a bartender for most of his life, and became the district manager for McKesson Liquor in Milwaukee until he retired shortly after his first heart attack at age 49. To him, accustomed to three-martini lunches, beer was a "chaser," or a beverage you drank when you wanted to sober up.

I was studying American lit at the time of his heart attack, and dropped by to see him in the hospital with a copy of Arthur Miller's *Death of a Salesman*. With a straight face, I gave him the book and told him he'd like it. He looked at me with that same you-gotta-be-kidding-me look he often gave me when I did or said something a bit odd. Maybe it was a poor choice, but I just finished reading it and seriously thought he'd like it. No, I don't think he read the book.

He died (1915-1990) before I got a chance to ask him his opinion of this country's crazed anti-pot hysteria that literally drives me to drink, and toke up! Every time I see another anti-alcohol ad on TV I feel like having a beer. I guess it's my O.D.D. (Oppositional Defiance Disorder) but damn, you can't even have a few beers without people thinking you're an alcoholic.

According to a recent study commissioned by a group trying to place restrictions on beer ads, the average child can name, and spell correctly, more brands of alcohol than presidents of the United States. That doesn't really surprise me, I mean, Coors and Bud are easier to spell than Roosevelt and Eisenhower.

When I was a kid my dad made me memorize "The Guckenheimer Song," which included the spelling of Guckenheimer (a blended whiskey) in the lyrics. It went something like "Good Old Guckenheimer/Smooth Guckenheimer/That's the brand for me..." Pretty bad, I admit.

"Hey Jimmy," dad would call, "Sing the Guckenheimer Song for your uncle Russell." And I'd sing to laughter and applause. Today this might appear to be child abuse to someone from the Parents' Temperance and Teetotaling Society, but back then it was just good fun. Not to mention educational, with a shot of male bonding thrown in.

Ironically, after leaving Milwaukee for California back in '69, I used to pass by this abandoned distillery just north of Sausalito on Bridgeway Avenue, not knowing what it really was until I was invited to read my poems at an informal reading of local poets. I was told the event was to be held at the old *Mason's Distillery*, producer of a brand of bourbon called Good Old Guckenheimer. It was destroyed by fire in 1963. Today it's the site of a condominium development called Whiskey Springs, or what a friend called, "Another egret displacement project."

Dad didn't want to hear me speak of the benefits of marijuana over those of alcohol, lumping all illegal drugs together, saying the "Dope pusher is the lowest form of humanity." This from a man who went from bartending to selling liquor for McKesson, one of the largest liquor and legal drug companies in the world. A man who spent all of his adult life pushing booze.

I'm not sure if my dad's nonchalant attitude about my teenage drinking encouraged me to be responsible, because once with my friends I was game to do almost anything. I certainly didn't drink responsibly by today's standards, yet I drank for the same reason kid's drink today—to party!

Back in the early 60s in Milwaukee County you had to be 21 to buy alcohol, but in most surrounding counties the minimum age was 18, so we used to drive the 20-30 miles to "teen bars," get loaded, and when the bars closed at 2.a.m. we'd drive back to Milwaukee—fast!

No seat belts. No designated drivers. No M.A.D.D or S.A.D.D. to spoil our fun, and no lame sayings like "Just Say No." "Just Do It!" was more our speed, though today it means buy overpriced footwear made in sweat shops in third-world countries.

When I was nineteen I was at my uncle Elmer's pickle farm, as we called it, and noticed an old Chevy in his garage. I asked what year it was and if he wanted to sell it. He said it was a 39' Chevy sedan and I could have it for $100. All it needed was a new battery, and off I went with my first automobile.

Friends used to beg me to double-date because it had a big, cushy back seat. Perfect for the drive-in movies. My buddy Dennis, who lived across the street, had a red '53 Chevy convertible, which we would take out to the teen bars, but when it came to going to the *Starlite Drive-In* on Route 41, he wanted me to drive so he could be in the back seat with his date.

Dennis and I worked as ushers at the local movie theater called *The Ritz,* a great place to meet chicks. And he was fun to pick up girls with because he always took the ugly one, figuring she "wanted it more." And hey, what can I say, she usually did. He had another theory, which I believe medical science eventually proved true, that the female ingestion of male sperm stimulates the growth of the mammary glands. Maybe I should do a fact-check?

One night we picked up our dates and cruised to the *Starlite Drive-In.* "I'll buy if you fly," I told him, and while he and his date were getting some popcorn, me and mine jumped in the back seat. They returned and got it on right in front of us. So much for that plan. Finally, after making more heavy breathing and gasping noises than really seemed necessary, the car suddenly stopped rocking and his head appeared above the seat, grinning, "How's the movie?"

Dennis has since gone through a few wives, at least two of them were devoutly religious, one to god and the other to astrology. I could never really understand the religious thing. I was raised Lutheran, but soon after I was confirmed I knew I'd had it with all that religious crap. When I told my Mom I didn't believe in god, she replied, "What do you believe in, communism!?"

"Let's just say I believe in everything you don't!" I said, before running up to my room.

Getting confirmed required attending catechism classes every Saturday morning. I hated going and soon devised a plan that worked out perfectly. The church was about four miles from our house, so my mom would give me money for the bus, which happened to be enough to buy a root beer float at the Carvel ice cream stand, which was about half-way to the church.

I would walk to Carvel, buy a treat and walk back home in approximately the same time it would take to attend catechism class by bus. And get a good workout too!

She never found out (I don't think), but I had a close call when at my confirmation, the pastor seemed to spend too much time giving me the evil eye. But just like teachers who hate to flunk kids because they don't want them in their class again, he confirmed me just to get rid of me. Good riddance.

My dad used to fall asleep in church so often that my mom finally let us both off the hook, requiring our attendance only at Christmas and Easter. We could live with that.

What dad couldn't live with was going without his daily martini, just as I hate to go without my evening brewski. Dad had several pet sayings, the one I liked best was, "I'd rather have a bottle in front of me, than a frontal lobotomy."

Spencer on his ketch, *Tenderly.*

That Other Drought

THE RECENT DROUGHT IN NORTHERN California made me think of the last one back in the mid-seventies when I was living on a friend's 20-acre property without electricity or running water. Actually, my friend, Spencer, didn't have any water, though he said he was going to drill a well and then build a water tower next to his driveway for gravity flow.

We ran into each other in the summer of '75 while in town getting showers at Quail Meadows, a campground and RV park just north of Willits run by Al and Marge, a nice English couple, that turned out to be a haven for the surrounding hill people who lived without indoor plumbing or running water, or as in Spencer's case, no water. He was filling up a couple barrels on the back of his flatbed truck when I caught his eye.

We both lived on sailboats at the Sausalito Gates in the early seventies, and shared the same old lady. Not at the same time, mind you, but after they broke up she seduced me. I was hanging around the campfire behind the *Ark*, an old paddle-wheeler called the *Charles van Damme* that was beached years earlier, and became a party boat, surrounded by a parking lot and the entrance to the infamous Gate 6 water squatters.

Suddenly this dark-haired beauty hands me a lit joint. We talked and soon ended up at the houseboat she was caretaking at Kappa's Yacht Harbor. It was a round two-story structure called the *Stone Soup*. The next morning I'm in this comfortable queen-sized bed with Jean, and we're about to go at it again when I hear somebody coming up the stairs.

"Oh, that's just Spencer. He ties his boat up here and uses my bathroom." She said it like it was no big deal. And there he was, smiling when he saw me in bed with his wife. Turns out they were still married, but he had only a friendly good morning for both of us. While he was in the bathroom I jumped up and got dressed. Jean cooked breakfast for both of us and we talked sailing.

It was a few months later, February '71, Jean and I were now living on my boat, the *Cowpie,* a 22-foot steel lifeboat that I bought in the summer of '69. It had the beginning of a small cabin and that's about it. Over the next few months I stepped in a mast, sewed some sails, had a two-foot long, half-inch thick steel keel welded on, and soon I was sailing around the Bay. Rather than pay a dockage fee, I stayed anchored out, using my little 8-foot dory to row back and forth to shore.

Jean said casually while making coffee, "Spencer's sailing down the coast today."

"Really!? Who's going with him?" I asked, but before I heard her answer I saw his boat, *Tenderly,* slowly inching toward us, him standing at the tiller, patiently drifting with the out-going tide. As he approached, he asked me if I wanted to go with him. He said he could sure use some help. He was going back to San Diego where he grew up, and said it shouldn't take more than four or five days.

Rather than wonder why my girlfriend's ex was inviting me to go sailing at the spur of the moment on a 26-foot sailboat with no engine, I thought instead, that sounds like an adventure, and said, "Okay, but I have to be back at work in four days." I had a part-time job at The Tides Bookstore in downtown Sausalito, and arranged it so I worked three straight days and then I'd be off for four, just so I could take off for short trips like this.

Spencer sailed in a circle, while I hauled up my 30-pound Danforth mud anchor. Jean took the tiller as I hoisted the sails. We sailed toward downtown Sausalito where I planned to anchor close to the entry to the Yacht Harbor so Jean would have an easier row to shore while I was away.

Pretty soon we were sailing under the Golden Gate Bridge and heading southwest. As the afternoon sun disappeared behind a mass of dark clouds approaching from the northwest, I asked Spencer what the weather forecast was, and he gave me a blank look, as if to say, *I knew I forgot something!*

As the evening darkened, the wind was picking up and the waves were getting bigger. Spencer decided to reef the main sail and hook up the storm jib. That may have been a life-saving decision, I thought later that night as a storm tossed our little 26-foot ketch around like a cork.

We took 4-hour shifts at the wheel, and hardly slept during our down time, with the wind howling and the waves crashing against the hull. At one point, while Spencer was down below trying to sleep, I saw whitecaps and waves breaking and figured we could be off-course and heading into some rocks, so I headed more west, which put more wind on the starboard side, causing the Tenderly to heel over even more, sending waves spraying on me, but figured I'd rather be wet and off-course than on the rocks.

In the morning when the storm broke there was hardly a breeze. Our now full sails were limp, so we just drifted down the coast on the Humboldt current. When Spencer came up on deck with a mug of coffee, he didn't like the fact that I went off-course, but he understood my fears, and like me was just happy we were still floating. We couldn't quite see land through a coastal fog that was slowly burning off, and we wanted to figure out where we were, so Spencer got out his *Coast Pilot*, a big atlas-size book with photos of the coast, including the longitudes and latitudes.

He figured we should be able to make it to San Simeon Bay by late afternoon, so I went down below and crashed. When we got to San Simeon Bay he decided with the weather so pleasant he could make it the rest of the way alone, so we tied up to a pier and found a little market, bought some supplies, and I hitchhiked back to Sausalito, spending the night on the Santa Cruz Boardwalk beach, then making it back to Sausalito in time for my next shift.

THE BIG SNOW OF FEBRUARY '75

When we ran into each other at Quail Meadows in '75 I told him we were looking for a place closer to town, and without a pause he offered his place. He suggested we get a trailer and park it next to this grassy meadow where his goats and chickens and ducks and a neighbor's horses hang out. I introduced him to Yvonne and our two-year old, Eli, which pleased him because he and his lady, Candy, also had a two-year old, Ida. Then I mentioned that we had two dogs, two cats and a donkey. He laughed when I told him the donkey's name was Don Quixote.

I told him we were renting a geodesic dome on the north slope of Shimmins Ridge, meaning, we hardly saw the sun all winter. When daylight came you knew that big orb was up there somewhere, but for most of November thru February not a ray of sunshine hit our house.

On sunny days I would take Eli for a hike to the sun, which was about a mile down the road on a south sloping meadow. He was always eager to go "find the sun," and toddled happily all the way. Then after playing in the warm sun for a while he'd sit on my lap and fall asleep. I'd put him in my *Snugli* and carry him back home. Yvonne would keep the woodstove going and cook us a nice hot meal from the bulk food we got in Willits once a month, and we'd take our afternoon nap.

Then one day in February it snowed more than a foot in just a few days, with drifts that changed the look of the landscape. We were running low on supplies so Yvonne talked me into going to town even though I couldn't see the road. My 1941 Dodge M-50 was 4-wheel drive, and this was the opportunity to test this World War II vehicle, so what the hell.

I got to the end of our quarter-mile driveway, where it turned slightly to the left… but I didn't, and drove into a 3-foot snow drift next to the road. Suddenly the truck tires were spinning and it slowly started tilting to the starboard side, so I turned it off and marveled at how different a familiar driveway looks covered by a couple feet of snow.

I was stuck and there was nothing I could do about it so I walked back up the hill. The old truck sat there for a month before I could move it, and every time Eli and I would walk past it on the way to the sun, he'd point and say, "Fruck! Fruck!" We still had her 1960 Volkswagon bus, but it wasn't going anywhere until the snow melted. What this all meant was I had to hike down the hill and hitchhike to town, filling my back pack with food, and return before dark.

Then the cold snap that followed the Big Snow ate up most of our firewood, leaving us wanting to be somewhere in the sun and closer to town, in a bad way. We both knew there was no way we'd spend another winter in that dome, or that we'd ever want to spend the winter on the north slope of any forest covered mountain!

Shortly after running into Spencer at Quail Meadows we bought an old 18-foot aluminum trailer called an *Alma*, copying the look of the more expensive *Airstream*, and moved it to his property. I built a 12 x 18-foot add-on with a Dutch door I made one-half at a time. We lived with just the bottom half for a while, until one day our bantam rooster, Gregory Pecky, perched on the door, eyes scouring the room in a threatening manner, or so I perceived, motivating me to finally build the top half of that door.

The scary part was he already had killed his dad, Johnny, and attacked me, jumping straight up, flapping his wings madly while he poked my knee with his talon. My knee was sore for a week, and all Yvonne would say is, "If you didn't act so macho around him he'd leave you alone."

One of my favorite memories was when Hoty, our donkey's nickname, would stand up to the door with his head inside ala Mr. Ed. And I wasn't the only one who talked to him. Another fond memory is when Yvonne would put Eli up on Hoty and walk them down the road, followed by the dogs, the goats, the cats, and sometimes the ducks, in that order. Birdie's three horses would join the parade too, if they were grazing nearby.

Birdie was a neighbor down the road who owned, besides the three horses, a huge hog and a white husky. Problem was Birdie was getting her vet degree from UC Davis, which required her to spend weekdays in Davis, leaving her horses, pig and large furry dog home alone. I don't think anyone was feeding these animals while she was away, which meant she left the food outside to share with the squirrels and the blue jays, and apparently the big dog didn't get enough. One day, Spencer came home telling me her dog chewed on the back of her pig.

"How do you know it was her dog?" I wondered.

"Come and see for yourself." We drove down the road and sure enough, the dog had blood all around his mouth and furry neck. Then we saw the pig. She had hunks of flesh chewed off her shoulders, bleeding and walking wobbly, making snorting noises with a scared look in her eyes. I remember saying to Spencer, "Gee, I like pork too, but this is going too far!"

The next thing I remember is Spencer pulling a rifle out from behind his truck seat, and looking at me with a *got any better ideas?* look. Bam, bam, and she went down on her front knees…bam, bam, …and she slowly toppled over. He then got out a chain and some rope. We tied her rear legs together and hung her upside down from an old oak tree, which didn't make Birdie too happy when she came home for the weekend to see her bloody hog hanging at the entrance to her driveway.

It wasn't long after the pig episode that Spencer and Candy split up and sold the property to Dick DeWitt, who didn't mind us being there as long as I helped him build a water tower, the one Spencer never got around to. After it was completed he had a *water dowser* come out and walk around following a Y-shaped twig (*divining rod?*) he held loosely in his hands, apparently waiting for the twig to point to water. DeWitt had two holes drilled where the *dowser* told him there was water, but no water. That's when I learned when you hire someone to drill for water, they don't guarantee water, just the hole. But what about the *dowser,* when does he get paid?

DeWitt also informed us, shortly after we finished building his water tower, that our trailer and add-on was actually on his neighbor's property. He told me that with a twinkle in his eye, but don't worry, he assured me, the owner lives in Santa Cruz and has no plans to build up here until after he retires.

For the year-and a-half we lived at Spencer's/DeWitt's we always got our water from Quail Meadows, but it wasn't because of the drought. Other parcels had water in their springs and wells, the city of Willits and Brooktrails Township had enough water, and it did finally rain late in '76, but only 15 inches for the year.

For me the drought ended when we finally had enough of no water and no electricity, and rented a real house in Brooktrails, which marked the first time I had been on the electrical grid since coming to California in '69, and the first time we had indoor plumbing (a shower and flush toilet!) since we'd been together in California. I liked it so much I decided to cut my hair, shave my beard, put on some shoes, and go back to school and get my teaching credential. So, that's what I went and done.

Me and cousin Marlene dancing at an older cousin's wedding.

The Warning 1967

Single men
beware of women
with wedding-cake smiles
for if they catch you
they will wrap their 33 1/3 rpm voice
around you
melt you to wax
label you MINE
and needle forever your High Fidelity.

Going Back to College Part 1

GOING BACK TO COLLEGE TO get my degree and a teaching credential after dropping out eight years earlier was tough in a lot of ways. The first was that the closest college from Willits was Sonoma State, nearly 100 miles south, which meant I had to go alone, leaving Yvonne and 3-year-old Eli at home from Sunday night to Friday evening. We didn't consider moving down to the Santa Rosa area, mostly because we just moved into our new rental, and had animals to take care of.

Another problem was if I was going to spend five nights a week in Sonoma County I needed to rent a room down there. This was January of 1977, before Sonoma State allowed student teachers to practice teach outside of Sonoma County, and before weekend seminars were enough to get a teaching credential.

Also, the credential program was designed to be three semesters long, two semesters of education classes and one of student teaching. Then I found out all I needed to graduate was one credit. Nearly a decade after dropping out I learn that all I need to get back in the rat race is one crumby credit. That one crumb was California History, which is required for all students in California.

I dropped out of the University of Wisconsin-Milwaukee back in January of 1969 with just one semester shy of getting my B.A. degree. I signed up for classes, but when the semester started I just didn't feel like going to school anymore. I had been going to school every year of my life since I was five years old. Enough! Plus, my personal life was in chaos. I had left my first wife, Lois, just before Christmas when I found out she was having an affair with a friend of a friend's friend. How did I find out? Well, four of us had taken LSD and we were sitting around our living room floor, *tripping*, when I noticed Lois holding hands with John. Suddenly it was clear, and without making a big fuss, I left.

I wasn't ready for marriage when we met two years earlier at a frat party, but after dating for a few months I suggested we live together, and she said, "That would kill my parents." So, half jesting, I said, "Well then, let's get married!" And she said, "Okay!" The exchange sounding more like kids playing in the backyard tree house.

Lois was a year older than me and was already teaching art at a suburban Milwaukee high school when we met, while I was in my fourth year of college, still needing two or more years to graduate because I transferred and changed majors a few times. I started out majoring in elementary education at Whitewater State College, but after a year I transferred to the Milwaukee Institute of Technology…the other MIT. Then after a year there I transferred to UWM, where I changed my major to PE, and finally to English.

I was also out for three sports—cross-country, wrestling, and track—combined with all the hours taking PE classes meant I spent way too much time in that funky old fieldhouse with other male jocks. I don't recall females having any collegiate sports at the time, unless you count cheerleading.

But it was the mid-sixties and the "times were a changin'." I had taken a poetry class with Barbara Gibson and got hooked, deciding to major in English, keeping PE as my minor. This of course pushed back my graduation date even further, now needing classes in Shakespeare, Chaucer, Structural Linguistics, and on and on. But the good news was I got to hang out with hip English majors—male and female--in the cozy basement cafeteria of the Downer Seminary, an extinct catholic girl's school the University had recently acquired.

English majors at UWM were required to take one year of a foreign language, but not at Sonoma State. Lois and I had hitched around Europe just the summer before, including from Paris to Marseille, and neither of us spoke anything but English and *Pig Latin*. The most trouble we had communicating was in Paris. It seemed that Parisians especially liked to make Americans struggle with their pretentious sounding language. I had read Sartre and Camus, and loved Bridget Bardot, so I was primed when I was told by someone in a matter-of-fact way, "English majors must take French."

The first semester back at UWM after travelling around Europe that summer of '68 started off okay, I mean, I got the classes I wanted, but Lois had quit teaching and had more time to hang with friends, and friends of friends. I had gotten a job in the campus bookstore to make ends meet, which didn't give me as much time to party as she had. She would often go out with a small group of mostly guys and get home late. When I found out and left I was invited to stay at Barbara Gibson's place, in her daughter's bedroom, while she was away at college.

Barbara and her husband Morgan both taught Creative Writing at UWM, and both were published poets who often invited other poets to come and read, usually followed by an informal get together at their place. Some of the poets who I met there were Allen Ginsberg, Robert Bly, Michael McClure, and Kenneth Rexroth. Rexroth, dubbed "The Father of the Beats" by Time Magazine, seemed old and burned out that evening, showering us innocent creative writing students in the Gibson's living room with his future vision of doom. When he finished he leaned his head back on his easy chair and shut his eyes while everyone in the room stayed eerily quiet, until finally I piped up, "Got any other good news for us?"

The muffled, knee-jerk laughter caused by my wise-ass comment made him slowly move his head back up and focus his glare at me, which slowly seemed to turn to pity, not just for me, but for other pathetic innocents like me.

VOULEZ VOUS COUCHER AVEC MOI?
The one class I was having trouble with was French, mostly because I wasn't studying, mostly because I decided I really didn't like French. To this day

all I remember is *oui* and *voulez vous coucher avec moi? (Yes,* and *will you go to bed with me?)* Luckily for me that my French teacher was an attractive blond who was nice enough to give me private lessons to get ready for the final exam.

One night sitting on her living room floor, cramming for the final while sharing a bottle of Merlot, I said those magic words that I still remember-- and *voila*, I suddenly had a new place to crash. Judy was two years older than me and working as a teacher's assistant, expecting to get her master degree in French by the end of the year, when I would get my BA. It was almost too easy, which made me wonder if I really wanted to get into another relationship.

The final came and went, and thanks to Judy's tutoring I passed with a C-minus. I signed up for my last semester, but as I said, I just didn't want to go. Then one night I was at my favorite bar, Hooligans, where draft beers were only 10 cents, and I ran into an old high school acquaintance, Bill Becker, who was living on a houseboat in Sausalito, California. Said he was heading back the next day and encouraged me to come check it out.

Becker was a pre-nerd in high school, meaning if there had been computers back then he would have had one. He hung with a small group of fellow pre-nerds who were in the *Projector Club.* They wheeled their projector equipment carts from classroom to classroom at the teachers' requests to show movies. Although he did end up getting into computers early on, and even running the computer department at a Honolulu Community College by the late nineties, that wasn't until he had lived a much more exciting life than the average nerd.

I'll quickly summarize his life from '68 to 2000. He rebuilt a three-wheeled motorcycle, drove it to California with his girlfriend Maggie in the side car, then bought a 30-foot flush deck sloop that had sunk in the Sausalito Yacht Harbor, rebuilt it and sailed to Hawaii and the South Seas. He sold the boat and bought property on the Big Island, built a house, watched the lava flow from the '83 Kilauea eruption slowly move toward it and sold it before it got devoured. Then moved to Oahu and got the computer job. The last time I talked to him was 2015, and when I asked him if he was still running the computer program for the college, he said, "No, now they pay me just to think."

I'd been wanting to go to California ever since reading the Beat Poets like Kerouac, Ferlinghetti, Corso, Ginsberg and Snyder, although my favorite beatnik was Maynard G. Krebs of the Dobie Gillis TV show. Besides Becker, I had another friend who had just moved to San Rafael, so now I knew two people I could visit. It was just days later that I decided to head west. I walked to nearby Downer Avenue, stuck out my thumb, and it started snowing, so I walked to the bus terminal and got on a bus to Madison for the first leg of my journey.

I talked the Sonoma State guidance counselor into combining my first two semesters into one, probably because I told her I had a pregnant wife and a three-year-old back in Willits. Oh yeah, I had just found out before leaving to restart my straight life that Yvonne was pregnant. She would be due sometime in September, when I was to start my student teaching.

The main reason I decided to go back to get my credential and teach and coach was because I had been working out at Willits High School with George Davis' wrestling team. He encouraged me to get my degree when I told him I had coached before back in Milwaukee while going to UWM, but dropped out in my last semester. He said he needed an assistant coach and he'd do all he could to help me get a teaching job at Willits High.

The week before classes started I was on campus buying some books and saw a *Roommate Wanted* ad on the cafeteria bulletin board, so for fifty bucks a month I rented a room in downtown Santa Rosa, and I was set to go. My drives back and forth were pretty much uneventful, which is a good thing, but one Friday afternoon I was driving my old '64 Chevy station wagon onto the Highway 101 freeway ramp heading north, when I saw a woman hitch-hiking, so I pulled over.

"Where you going?" I asked the aging hippie chick, as she sashayed over to my window, smiling, and replied, "Nowhere in particular, sweetie, I'm working."

My first response was to play dumb and ask, "What do you do?" But instead I asked, awkwardly, "How much do you charge?"

"Twenty bucks," she replied, sounding as if she was giving me a discount. But just then a big truck was coming up behind me, so I quickly apologized, telling her I was broke, and took off. Looking in my rearview mirror I noticed the truck stop and she got in. As I continued north I saw that my gas gauge was near empty and when I stopped in Ukiah for gas I found a twenty dollar bill in my wallet, and that's all I had. I felt a little better knowing that if I had donated twenty bucks to the charming roadside hooker, my car would have died about halfway home, which helped convince me that I had made the right decision.

Alone on Sonoma Beach

for Judy

Boot prints along the beach end here
A bone-white log for shelter
I clear a spot in the sand for my sleeping bag
Wind at my ears.
2000 miles away you pop pills to stay awake
Study French History
Open a window for fresh air.

Going Back to College Part 2

MY FIRST SEMESTER WAS OVER and now I needed a summer job. I had worked on the Mendocino County road crew out of the Laytonville Yard the past two seasons as part of the C.E.T.A crew that built the two-mile path along Branscomb Road in '75, then hired back as a grunt in '76, mostly digging out culverts, cutting back brush, and flagging, the most boring job there is. But when I heard the County was hiring out of the Ukiah Yard, I forgot all that and went for an interview.

Turned out they had already hired a crew but still needed a crew leader. My two years in Laytonville was enough to convince the yard boss that I was the man for the job, and was told to start the following Monday.

I had a motley crew of five, including two women. One always had her favorite designer gloves, and the other wore colorful tie-dyed shirts, arguing that they were more visible and therefore safer on the road than the red vests they issued.

Then there was a local Pomo Indian who I don't remember saying much; a typical white guy like me who just wanted to work, and within a year or so I saw him flagging for Cal Trans; and an Afro-American who had come to Redwood Valley from Indiana in the sixties with the Jim Jones *Peoples' Temple cult*, but defected when they moved to San Francisco the year before. It was the next year on November 18, 1978 that 918 people at Jonestown, Guyana died from drinking the cyanide-laced Kool Aid.

One thing I learned on that job was if I wanted to get any work done, I couldn't just tell them what do, lean on a shovel and watch them work, I had to work too, which I really didn't mind. We actually had a good time and I was sorry that I would have to quit early to start my student teaching. And the way I did it, without any notice, just a phone call to a message machine, meant no more county jobs for me. Quitting a month or so before being laid off also meant no unemployment income all winter, something I always liked about seasonal jobs.

I was to start my student teaching at El Molino High School in Forestville, a little town west of Santa Rosa, when the semester started the week after Labor Day, and I still didn't have a place to stay down there, but that turned out to be serendipitous. I went to a neighbor's party and met an attractive single mother who told me she lived in Cotati, which was just west of Rohnert Park, where Sonoma State was located. I told her I needed a place to stay from Sunday night to Friday morning and she offered me her bedroom for $50 a month, saying nonchalantly, "I'll just sleep with my daughter those nights." Problem solved.

As the summer wore on, Yvonne really started to bulge, and I hated to leave her behind in her last month of pregnancy, but she supported me, no doubt wanting me to get my degree and a real job even more than I did. She had everything worked out so she wouldn't have to deliver the baby in the local hospital. We had taken birthing classes together, her belly-dancing partner, Jeannie, offered her living room floor, Maria, a self-proclaimed mid-wife would help, and local artist, Linda, would shoot a home movie. What could possibly go wrong?

Knowing I would have no income from September until January or so, I had gotten together with local Willits middle school PE teacher Tom Tilton to take a wrestling officials course, which required us to spend a few Saturdays in Santa Rosa.

Tilton was probably the best thing that ever happened to the troubled Baechtel Grove Middle School, where I ended up teaching 6th grade for the '83-84 school year. And the community agreed, renaming the

Baechtel Grove Middle School's community-used gym the Tom Tilton Gymnasium, upon his recent retirement after nearly 40 years at that one school.

I was mostly assigned to officiate dual meets in the Santa Rosa area, but just before Christmas break I was to ref a dual meet at Willits High School. I admit I was a little nervous to referee in Willits for the first time, but had much respect for coach George Davis, for many reasons, the main one was that I was there and about to graduate with a teaching credential mostly because of his encouragement. Also, because I liked the way he seemed to *think outside the box*. However, I soon found out he may have thought too far outside the box.

Everything was going fine until I stopped a middle-weight match because the Willits wrestler's nose started bleeding a bit too much while trying to pin his opponent. The blood was running onto the wrestler's face, neck, and uniform. I blew my whistle, gave the Willits wrestler three points for a near-pin, but George exploded, coming on to the mat yelling that I should not have stopped it because neither wrestler was in physical danger, as if bleeding profusely from the nose is okay. I couldn't believe he was doing this to me, I mean, his team was ahead, as was his wrestler. What was his point? Was this one of his *lessons*?

I was suddenly glad that Bob Colvig, a recent grad from Chico State, and a Willits High alumnus, had just been hired to teach business, and became George's new assistant wrestling coach. I'm pretty sure he also encouraged Bob to come back to Willits and be his assistant coach, and that I was more or less *plan B*.

That was okay with me because I had started running while going to Sonoma State, and eventually got a teaching job in the Willits district, and coached the high school cross-country and track teams.

THE START OF STUDENT TEACHING
I was assigned to teach three English classes for the entire semester, one of which was Reading, taught by Ron Elder who also happened to be the

wrestling coach, and a successful one. We made a deal that if I helped coach his team after school two days a week I wouldn't have to teach his 9th grade Reading class, but could just sit in the back and observe them read. We didn't really make that deal, but that's the way it turned out, except for Friday's when he let me give the spelling tests.

My second class each day was Composition, with master teacher Mike Miller, who stressed grammar, structure, and classroom discipline. And-- surprise!!--he was also the football coach. Early on he told me I seemed to be "floating, pulling ideas out of the air," and instructed me to have my "assignment decided on beforehand, don't make it up during class."

I wanted to teach them how to write a clearly understood paragraph, and they even agreed that it would be nice to write something that could be read and understood. I never liked grammar and assumed they didn't like it either.

Then I was absent for a few days during Riley's coming out party, and Miller asked them for suggestions on how to improve the class. I was surprised at some of them, such as: 1) more grammar; 2) more assignments; 3) more grades. I couldn't help but wonder if they would have given the same suggestions if I had asked them. So, I gave them my own questionnaire: What do you like most and what do you like least about this class?

Three of the answers I received for both questions were: grammar, writing, and nothing. The class was split, some wanted more grammar because they didn't want to write, and others liked writing and hated grammar. I had played down grades, but since they wanted them I devised a point system and kept close track of their points. Then when I gave them an assignment the most often asked question was, "How many points do we get?"

Jan Stevens was my master teacher in American Literature, but I jokingly called her my "mistress teacher." She was nice enough to have another desk brought in just for me, and made me feel free to come and go anytime. She always listened to me and had something positive to say. She never failed to make me feel like I belonged, that I had a lot to offer these kids.

One of the real eye-openers was when I had the class videotaped. I don't remember whose idea it was, but showing it back to the students, asking for comments, and the honesty in the ensuing discussions was more like a therapy session. From then on they never hesitated to tell me when it got boring.

Riley's Home-Birth

My new landlady was really sweet, and made my stay at her two-bedroom apartment feel more like a guest than a part-time tenant. One night after her six-year-old daughter fell asleep, we were sitting around having a glass of wine and I was telling her about the tai chi classes I had taken. She was interested in learning the basics, so I told her to do what I was doing. I stood up and got in a relaxed position to *find my center,* then slowly started moving to show her some of the *form.* Then I walked over to help her, while telling her to breathe in through her nose and out through pursed lips. I instructed her to tuck her pelvis and chin, and raise her chest, while lightly touching these areas.

If this had been a date I felt like we would soon be all over each other, so I decided it was time to say good night, and went to bed. About twenty minutes later, she tapped lightly on the door and softly wondered if I wanted to "snuggle."

Some questions deserve only one answer. She slipped between the sheets, and when we finished *snuggling,* she crept back to her daughter's room. I laid there feeling really good, and maybe a little bit guilty. I fell asleep until the phone rang about an hour later. It was Yvonne telling me her water broke and she was already at Jeannie's starting to go into labor.

I hit the road, and by early morning on September 30 I was sitting on Jeannie's floor, leaning against her couch, Yvonne's back against me and her legs spread wide, grunting and pushing until the baby's head crowned and slowly emerged, then plop, out came this healthy boy we named Riley James Gibbons.

As for Linda's home birthing movie, we used to show it every year at Riley's birthday parties so all his friends could see where babies really come from. I'm kidding! I never saw it or wanted to see it…until now, as I write this, I suddenly have an interest in seeing it, yet something tells me my interest will soon wane.

ALMOST A BIG DEAL

Missing classes for a few days was no big deal, but my next adventure very well could have been a big deal if it weren't for some nice person who I never got to thank. The mid-term was over and I placed all the completed tests and make-up homework into a folder with my grade book. I had taken 4-year-old Eli with me that week because it was minimum-day week, and I wanted to spend more time with him, plus give Yvonne a break.

On Friday, I picked him up from the nearby day care center before heading back to Willits, but what I didn't realize until I got home was that my folder was missing. My grade book with all the mid-term exams, make-up homework, and everything...gone! And I had no back-up. Suddenly I was in deep *feces*. I mentally retraced my steps after leaving school, and realized I had placed the folder on the roof of the car to strap Eli into his car seat, then drove off.

To top it off, the next week I was to be evaluated by my Sonoma State educational supervisor, Dr. Elliot. My future in education didn't look too promising. Then I got a phone call from the Cotati Police Department, telling me that someone brought in a folder they found a few miles east of Forestville with my name on it. I was saved by someone I never got to thank, but in case you're reading this, thanks.

The day of my evaluation, instead of doing the standard teaching thing, I told the story of my lost folder, and stretched it out a bit as the students seemed to be really interested for a change. Dr. Elliot seemed impressed enough to give me a very positive evaluation and told me I was doing just fine.

Everything went smoothly from then on, and in the last week a student asked me if I was going to be back next semester. I told her no, I'd be heading back to Willits. Another student asked if I would stay if they offered me a job. I said, yes, I probably would. They buzzed together and said they would "start a petition to get me hired," which embarrassed me and I quickly discouraged them. When I told this story to a fellow student teacher, she said, "You should have let them do it, it would look great on your resume."

Alotta Lipski

It was my very first sixth-grade faculty meeting at Little Lake Valley Middle School. There were just four of us, all men, but we were waiting for one more teacher before we could proceed. That teacher was Alotta Lipski, a transfer from the local elementary school, whose no-nonsense reputation had these guys worried, and they were trying to agree on how to handle her.

I didn't say much, except her name out loud, slowly, "A-lot-ta Lip-ski?" And just then, as if on cue, the door opened and she marched in, slammed her load of books on the table, and sat down, as if to say, "Okay, dickheads, let's get this over with, I have more important things to do!"

She was attractive, in a tight-lipped, stern-squint sort of way. Pete, the more experienced of the crew, started the meeting by introducing her to me, the other new teacher. She gave me a curt, non-judgmental hello, and looked back at Pete, prompting him to get on with it.

I decided she had a nice body, what I could imagine under that below-the-knee-length skirt, and long-sleeved, buttoned-up-to-the-neck blouse. I mean, it was still August and the temperature outside was pushing 100 degrees!

When the meeting was adjourned she was the first out the door. I lingered because I had questions, but mostly because, unlike my room, Pete's was air-conditioned. My air-conditioner was "being fixed." Being fixed, I soon learned, was the district's equivalent of "the check's in the mail."

The other male teachers congratulated Pete on his handling of Alotta, which noticeably pleased him. The few things she did say during the meeting were direct and to the point. She got what she wanted and left. After which I learned that she had been married to a fifth-grade teacher at this school, but got divorced last year after he'd been seen too often with one of the lunch aides, a tough born-and-raised local who always seemed pissed off at someone, and naturally took it out on the kids.

I spent that afternoon trying to get my room ready for the first day of school the following Monday. I was knee-deep in out-dated text books and useless art supplies when the door opened, and there stood Alotta, smiling at me.

"Hey, it's three o'clock, break time." She walked in and handed me a Pepsi, said she doesn't drink alcohol, but has a six-pack-a-day Pepsi habit. "Everybody has a weakness, right?" She winked seductively, adding, "What's yours?"

"Mine is teaching sixth-grade," I said, sounding a bit too serious. She offered her help in "any way possible," and gave me two teacher tips, which didn't sink in right away:

1) Don't take any work home you can finish at school, and
2) Don't smile until Thanksgiving.

The first day of school was much like a bad dream. I had thirty-five kids bouncing off the walls. Some were repeating 6th grade for "emotional reasons." One kid was taller than me and looked about fifteen. Turned out he had never been "mainstreamed" before. I was told later that the 5th grade teachers who passed these feral kids on to me figured I could handle them because I had taught "troubled kids" in the local continuation school (my first job in the district).

I complained to Alotta, who slowly became my invaluable sixth-grade guide, and after reading my class list, informed me that I was "dumped on." She taught fourth grade in the district for the past ten years and knew most of these kids, their older brothers and sisters, parents and guardians.

"The new teacher always gets dumped on," she said, taking a swig of Pepsi while scanning my class list, "But they really STUCK it to you!"

"Great," I deadpanned, "A challenge, just what I needed."

She then summed up my attendance list: "Some of these kids should be put back in Special Ed, some should be split up, and a few should be sent to reform school--and the sooner the better!" She laughed, and added, "This is more than a "challenge," it's a cheap shot by them (the 5th grade teachers), and a survival test for you!"

Somehow, even though I was dumb enough to smile on the first day of school, and even took work home, I got through that first semester. It wasn't easy, but I learned a lot, even though it was often "the hard way." It got to the point where the class was willing to help me write up a list of rules. I was surprised how strict their rules were compared to mine, but then I realized they wanted to spend way too much time policing each other, as in, "Joey wrote on my paper!"; "Troy broke his pencil on purpose!"; "Lynda said the F-word!"

I was tired of this continual battle to keep order, of always being the stern teacher, constantly being tested, pushed. I didn't want to keep them in for recess or after school--why should I be punished? Then there were those rare days I sensed I taught them something. I mean, it had to happen, right? To see their eyes light up and have them thank me in so many kind-hearted ways—NOT!

Truth is, the job was so stressful and demanding that some days the 3:05 bell would ring and I'd just sit there staring at the papers stacked on my desk, wishing like hell I didn't have to return the next day and do it all over again. I took the job home with me every night like an incurable disease. I felt no freer than those guys from the county jail on work furlough—only I was sure they were having more fun.

Halloween and Valentine's Day are good examples of the worst days for a new teacher. The kids come to school loaded on sugar and caffeine. It's a war zone. You can't let your guard down for a second. You can't even show a movie because they'll go nuts as soon as you turn off the lights.

The big craze that school year was Jolt, a cola with "all the sugar and twice the caffeine!" Just what these kids needed! They'd come in from lunch wired to the max on Jolt and candy. This is when I wished I were the PE teacher. Make them run around the playground for a while.

I eventually whittled the class size down to a manageable twenty-six, splitting up the trouble-makers as Alotta suggested, sending one to the school psychologist, and the big kid back to Special Ed. The school psychologist, by the way, enjoyed observing my class. She thought it was a lively bunch, and said I was "Doing a good job, though a bit unconventional, keeping the kids interested in learning."

Lucky for me she was sitting in the back of the classroom the day Aimee came in and wouldn't leave, even after I asked her politely. She kept talking to her friend Lynda until the bell rang. I told her again to leave, but she ignored me and continued to converse. I walked toward her with my grade book held stiff-armed, literally pushing her slowly out the door.

Aimee was originally in my class with her best friend Lynda, but Alotta had suggested I transfer the clique leader to Pete's class. I had to choose who was the alpha dog in this group? I decided it was between Aimee and her friend Lynda. I chose Aimee, but soon learned that Lynda was the real alpha dog, but she had a weakness—Michael Jackson's new *Thriller* album. She not only cooperated with me all week if I would let them hear *Thriller* on Friday afternoon, but actually helped keep order. Not even the boys would disobey Lynda.

But back to Aimee's forced exit. Before the day was over I was told to report to the principal's office after school to meet Aimee's mother. I made sure the school psychologist also attended. Aimee was crying when she told her story, describing how I had my "hands all over" her. What she didn't realize was that the psychologist had been sitting in the back row observing the whole scene.

When Aimee finished her story, the psychologist described what really happened, pointing out that both my hands were clutching my grade book, proving they could not have been "all over" her. Furthermore, she reported that she was appalled at Aimee's rudeness and disrespect.

When Aimee's mother realized her precious daughter had been lying, she gave her an I'll-deal-with-you-later look, apologized to me and the principal, and made a quick exit.

Why did the school psychologist come to observe me? At first it was at my request to see if she could help size-up the situation, possibly give me some helpful hints. She returned out of curiosity, telling me once, "You can't duplicate this experiment in a laboratory."

She was partly referring to my Teacher-Student Day. I would choose a volunteer to teach a lesson for say, five to 10 minutes. Some were better than others, but the best part was usually the question and answer session afterward. She liked their enthusiasm, and we both agreed they were easier on each other (and me) after they took turns teaching in front of each other. In fact, it seemed to improve the overall behavior of the class, an unexpected plus.

Things were going much smoother the second semester, in fact, better than I had anticipated. We seemed to be co-existing on a rather relaxed set of rules, as if everyone agreed to get along and work together to actually learn something (this time I'm not kidding!).

Few nights went by without Alotta calling me and crying about the latest fight she had with Rick. He couldn't be as bad as she made him out to be, could he? She said his lunch-aide girlfriend went as far as threatening her physically! Although Alotta and Rick own property west of town, she had recently rented her own apartment in town, and taking custody of their two children. Although we were warming up to each other in private, at school she was business-as-usual, preferring to eat in her own room instead of the teachers' lounge.

I looked forward to the teacher's lounge, a chance to get away from the kids for a half-hour, and spend that precious time with grown-ups. What I learned in the teachers' lounge, besides the usual scuttlebutt, was a new respect for sixth-grade teachers, especially those who embraced teaching and couldn't see themselves doing anything else. As for the old saying- *-Those who can, do; and those who can't, teach--*I now believe is an unfair put-down.

I'm sure there were plenty of competent teachers at Little Lake Valley, although they did lose a few back in the mid-70s when the Supreme Court outlawed paddling. I was astonished to discover that some of the teachers I was working with actually used to paddle their students!

"And it worked," volunteered Roy, who quit teaching the year they made paddling illegal, and now drives truck for Coca Cola. Roy just happened to be filling the Coke machine in the lounge, a job he does once a week. "Oh, I had to get another teacher to witness it. We couldn't just hit them when they were bad, like you do with your own kids. I mean, some teachers did, and that is the best way to train the little brats, but you had to protect yourself. Yes, paddling was effective," Roy concluded.

"I wouldn't support a system that gave adults the freedom to physically abuse children," a young female teacher said, as if speaking her turn in a Philosophy of Education class.

"Yeah, but it sure felt good, huh Roy?" An old-timer cracked, causing mild laughter.

Roy smiled and said snidely, "No, we didn't get paid to go to all these educational seminars to learn the latest classroom management skills and self-esteem techniques." He turned his dolly of empty coke bottles around and headed for the door, adding, "The rule in my classroom was Fear the Paddle! And it worked!"

Spring came and I started counting the days until summer vacation, but first the annual field trip. As all Little Lake sixth graders knew, spring is the time for the annual Nature Conservancy Field Trip. The Nature Conservancy is in Branscomb, an hour's ride north, deep in a Redwood forest. The field trip needed parents to help chaperone, as we would be spending two nights in small cabins, while daytime was reserved for various learning activities.

Things were going fine the first day, so while the students had some rest time before dinner I decided to go for a run. I notified one of the other teachers that I might be gone for up to an hour, and took off.

I got back to find out while I was gone one of the chaperone mothers, I'll call her Lynda's Mom, had started a fight with another mother!

Well, almost a fight. Lynda's Mom pushed the other mother, and the other mother backed down to avoid fisticuffs. I don't remember what pissed them off, but it just might have inspired a few kids into causing a mild ruckus later that evening.

The highlight of the trip to many students had long been the night hike to the "Haunted House." The Haunted House was an old abandoned two-story Victorian that hadn't been lived in for years. The Nature Conservancy counselors traditionally take the students on this night hike to the "Haunted House" after telling them of the local rumors that the house is haunted. When they get there, they walk around the wrap-around deck looking in the windows for ghosts.

Turned out that two 6th graders (not from my class!) broke into the house before we got there and caused an uproar, running around making scary noises, which got everyone in a tizzy and obviously pissed off the counselors, resulting in the Conservancy people deciding that the field trip experience for Little Lake Middle School had come to an end, and that turned out to be the last Nature Conservancy Field Trip for our school since.

As the school year came to a close, Alotta and I discovered that our birthday was on the same day—June 15th. I was a few years older, but the coincidence was such that we knew we had to celebrate together. We dined at a popular steakhouse in Redwood Valley, and afterward, in the parking lot, made out for the first time. I was in heaven. I had found the woman of my dreams, but when I took her home she suddenly turned cold and wouldn't invite me in or even kiss me good night.

We had stopped for gas on the way home, and unbeknownst to me she had purchased a Playboy magazine. When we got to her apartment she said goodnight and tossed the Playboy at me, explaining: "To help you cool down and go to sleep."

"Thanks," I deadpanned, feeling suddenly like a teenager again.

Well, I did get the transfer to the high school and was looking forward to the new school year, a new cross-country season, and perhaps down the line a new girlfriend.

__POSTSCRIPT__*: The only name I changed in this story is Alotta Lipski, whose real name was Alpha Lipman. A short time later she took the kids and moved to Wisconsin. I never heard from her again.*

Teacher, You Have A Heart On

My first day at Willits High School was not what I expected, though I'm not sure just what my expectations were, other than to have a homeroom and a mix of literature and writing classes. Well, I had no lit or writing classes, just 8th, 9th and 10th grade Basic English, meaning they were not college bound, and as I soon found out, not very bound to graduate from high school either. What the heck, I just spent a year teaching 6th grade, how hard could this be?

The other disappointment was that I didn't have a homeroom. They didn't have enough rooms in the old school building or even enough boxes out back called "portables," so I had to tote everything from class to class, using different teachers' classrooms while they were on their breaks.

The good news of not having a homeroom was that when other teachers and their students were in homeroom, listening to the daily announcements and saying the Pledge of Allegiance, I was free to have a cup of coffee in the cafeteria, or hang out in my little library cubicle that Diana, the sweet school librarian, let me use during my free time.

It happened in my 9th grade class after lunch. I was standing in front of the room, grade book in hand, waiting for the final bell (the first bell is the five-minute warning). It rang and I started to introduce myself when a young girl came in, apologized for being late, walked up to me and stuck a little red heart on my shirt pocket. Yes, a bit odd, but she then sat down and raised her hand. I played along and said, "Yes?"

She said, in a sing-song voice, "Teacher, you have a heart on."
I looked down on my shirt and responded, "I see that, and I thank you for giving it to me," which caused the class to laugh and giggle, as "heart on" sounded a lot like "hard-on." I suppressed any acknowledgement of the coincidental sound likeness, and continued to take roll call.

In case you're wondering what happened to the precocious young lady, she dropped out of school in mid-semester, and some years later was seen dragging two young ones down Main Street, followed by a homeless looking dude called Daddy by one of the youngsters. What does this teach us? Stay in school!

My fourth period class, just before lunch, was in George Davis' classroom, one of the portables way out back by the track. Talk about basic, his class had no frills, nothing on the bulletin boards, no cutesy wall hangings or inspirational messages, just a blank blackboard (it was actually green), one piece of chalk, and one eraser.

I mention this because one day I dismissed the class, gathered my stuff, and headed to my little nook in the library. I no sooner sat down when suddenly George Davis appeared with his hand out, and said, tersely, "Chalk?" I had absentmindedly put his only piece of chalk in my pocket. He had walked across campus, leaving his classroom waiting, while he retrieved his only piece of chalk. Lesson learned, I never walked off with his only piece of chalk again.

I should mention that besides teaching English, George Davis was the wrestling coach at the high school, but more than that he was a sort of local legend. He had taught and coached football at St. Helena years before where his teams went five years without a loss!

From 1960-64 they amassed a record of 45 wins and no losses! And the kicker was, he let his players make the decisions of who would play what positions and which plays to call. His democratic coaching methods attracted a *New York Times* reporter named Neil Amdur, who ended up writing a book about George's coaching methods called *The Fifth Down*. You can get it at the Mendocino County Library.

George moved to Willits to teach English and coach football, but his unusual coaching methods didn't work here, and after a few losing seasons he retired from coaching football and turned to wrestling. He had a remarkable run coaching wrestling at Willits High, considering that he never wrestled himself and only learned the sport after he took over the team.

I should also mention that the reason I went back to school to get my teaching credential was because of George. Back in 1976 I wanted to get back in shape, so I used to drop in a few days a week and work out with his wrestling team. He liked my "manner" with the kids, and some of my moves that he hadn't seen before. One in particular was the whizzer, that he renamed the "Wisconsin Carry," after I mentioned that I wrestled and coached in Wisconsin back in the Sixties.

When I told him I was an English major, planning to teach and coach, but dropped out of college my last semester and moved to California, he encouraged me to go back to school and get my teaching credential. He said he really needed an assistant coach, and that he'd do all he could to help me get a teaching job at the high school.

So I went to Sonoma State University for the Spring semester of '77 to find out I only needed a one-credit course in California History to graduate. But I also needed some education classes, and a full semester of student teaching to get my credential.

This story might sound better if I had returned to Willits a year later with my degree and credential, got hired to teach English and became his assistant coach, eventually taking over the team to lead them to a winning record for many years before finally retiring to live happily ever after.

Yes, that actually happened, but not to me. I did, in fact, return in January, 1978 with my degree, only to discover that Bob Colvig (Willits class of '66) had returned from Chico with his teaching degree, becoming George's new assistant coach, and eventually lived out the above scenario.

But that was fine with me because I had started running while going to Sonoma State, and the running craze took hold. I kept putting in more mileage and within a year of serious training, ran my first marathon (Napa Valley) in 2 hours and 55 minutes, that qualified me to run the prestigious Boston Marathon, which I did in 1980.

I still remember my last work out with the team, shortly after returning in '78. A likable kid named Pat Page, who I had wrestled with when he was a 120-pound Sophomore, again when he was a 140-pound Junior, and now he's a 160-pound Senior, while I'm still at 130.

After he over-powered me to get the takedown, he wrapped his arm around my waist and squeezed as I tried to escape...crack! We both heard it, and afterward I told George that I was training for a marathon and didn't need to get on the mat with these kids anymore. He understood, making me feel good about my decision, saying something like, "There are so many things we have to do every day, it doesn't make any sense to do what we don't want to if we don't have to..." Or something like that.

Meanwhile, back in '84 at the high school I was miserable. After five years in the district teaching at the continuation school, and the previous year at the middle school, I finally got to the high school and realized I was burned out. I wondered what I'd do for money if I actually quit. What some teachers do when they get burned out in the classroom is get a job as a counselor or administrator. The credentials were easy enough to get, a few weekends at some retreat in Sonoma, a mail order exam, and voila! they've rid themselves of those pesky kids.

Over the years I knew more than a few teachers who became Vice Principals and Principals, making hell more money than they did in the classroom. But I'd had it, I didn't want any of those jobs, and knew I had to submit my resignation before the Christmas vacation so I wouldn't be stuck till the end of the year.

On the last day of class before the two-week vacation I told Principal Chuck Davidson that I'd "lost my enthusiasm for the job." He suggested I take a sabbatical, but that would mean finishing out the school year, which I didn't want to do. He told me to "put it in writing." I went home and wrote the following:

> *I am submitting this letter of resignation to go into effect January 18, 1985 (the last day of the current semester). My reason for this difficult decision is due to a recent lack of enthusiasm, and a worsening depression that, I believe, is directly related to the stress of teaching semi-literate, unmotivated, and too often disrespectful students...* You get the idea.

I missed my retirement party because I contracted a mean case of flu that knocked me down for a few weeks, but I was a free man with nearly $7,000 owed to me by the teacher's retirement system. Life looked good and when I recovered I went to Mexico with a few friends to celebrate.

Have I ever regretted my decision to quit teaching?

Not yet...

Seeking The Sunny Mexican Cure

I DIDN'T SEEM TO BE recovering from my viral pneumonia in Willits, in fact, when my friends Chris and Donna called to invite me along to Mexico I was in the throes of a relapse. I had just been to Baechtel Creek Clinic to find out why I felt even worse after one week of religious doses of Erythromycin.

Dr. Glyer listened to my breathing and announced that I had more fluid in my lungs now than a week ago. He took some blood and sent me to Howard Hospital for chest X-rays. The X-rays revealed that both lungs contained fluid, and even showed a few calcified spots from past bouts with pneumonia.

I was depressed. I couldn't take a deep breath without coughing. I couldn't run. I couldn't drink beer. And now it looked like I couldn't go to Mexico! Besides that, I had quit my teaching job and my benefits would run out in two days.

The good news, however, was that the reason the Erythromycin didn't work is because I had had a viral pneumonia, but now in my weakened state, apparently a bacteria had taken over my lungs, and penicillin was specially *molded* for the job!

My friends were leaving in four days—would I be fit enough to go? It was all up to the Wonder Drug.

Donna called back Saturday to find out my progress. "Yes, yes," I wheezed, "buy my ticket. I'm going." I was taking a risk, but I decided I'd rather be sick on a beach in Mexico, than in the winter chill of Willits.

We left San Francisco Monday morning, February 4. I had my American Express Travelers checks, my Coppertone lotion, and my penicillin. Nothing else seemed very important.

Not having purchased the standard Puerto Vallarta tour package, naturally I was somewhat anxious to find a hotel room soon after our arrival. Dragging my diseased lungs through the dusty streets, searching for a hotel room was not my idea of the sunny Mexican cure. I harbored visions of coughing myself to sleep on the beach while a gang of gnarly desperadoes lingered in the shadows, trading exotic drugs for shiny weapons.

The confidence that I could run to escape from impending physical harm has been my security blanket ever since I was a skinny kid, but with my lungs out of commission I was forced to rely on the safety-in-numbers theory—being just one of the helpless flock of milquetoast tourists trying to stay out of harm's way.

El Presidente Miguel de la Madrid periodically admonishes his people to be nice to tourists, and everyone seems friendly enough, but horror stories do crop up. People abducted off the streets, a couple murdered on the beach, and American sailboats harassed near the *Islas Tres Marias*, the "Prison Islands," fifty miles northwest of Puerto Vallarta.

According to the boating magazine, *Latitude 38*, men heavily armed with M16s boarded a Ventura couple's boat, searched it thoroughly, and delayed them for hours just because they sailed too close to the Islands.

The magazine goes on to say, "There are 5,000 to 6,000 prisoners on the islands, most of them drug smugglers. Eye witnesses say that some of the prisoners are tied to stakes and left in the sun. They don't coddle prisoners in Mexico; in fact, some folks say they simply lose track of who is in there."

Our friend Roy had stayed in the Rosita last year, but some how we translated Rosita to Rosarita, no doubt due to eating too many cans of Rosarita brand refried beans. The taxi driver looked at us blankly, repeating "Rosarita? RosaREETa?" Then his eyes got big, "RoZEETa! RoZEEta!"

The Rosita was full, but they were building a new hotel down the street called *El Pescador*. As we walked toward this new hotel, my body and spirits sagging, I thought of the young American who shared our bus ride to town. He didn't lift my spirits much when he cautioned us about the latest malaria outbreak.

"Just what I need," I had said wryly, "Double malaria on top of double pneumonia! I guess I'll let them fight it out!"

The most noticeable thing about this town, besides the constant stream of taxis grinding over the cobblestone streets, is the construction. It's not hard to believe that this is the fastest growing seaside resort in North America, but it is hard to believe that this modern-day paradise was a quaint little fishing village without electricity, telephones, or roads to the outside world before 1960. Sandwiched between the Sierra Madre Mountains and the Pacific Ocean, a twice-a-week flight from Guadalajara, 225 miles to the northeast, was its main connection to the outside world.

Then Liz Taylor and Richard Burton had their shocking love affair while filming *Night of the Iguana,* and suddenly Puerto Vallarta was put on the map.

Puerto Vallarta on 5,000 Pesos a Day

El Pescador turned out to be what the travel brochures might call "The best kept secret in Puerto Vallarta!" This brand spanking new four story hotel, perched right on the beach, was just 5,000 pesos a night, or $22.72 at the current exchange rate of 220 pesos on the relatively strong dollar.

We got a large room that slept four comfortably, including firm mattresses, a working telephone, plenty of hot water, and an unnatural lack of insects. Even when I switched on the bathroom light in the middle of the night there were no *cucarachas* scurrying for cover. And not one fly or mosquito buzzed my ear the whole time. This was absolutely unheard of in any tropical paradise I'd ever been before. And then one afternoon I found out why.

A knock on the door interrupted my mid-afternoon siesta, and I opened it to see a man standing in the hallway with a large ominous tank strapped to his shoulder, and a long nozzle in his hand. He said just one word I understood, "SPRAY!"

"NO SPRAY! NO SPRAY!" I said weakly, backing away slowly. He disregarded my feeble plea, stepped into the room and walked straight to the bathroom shower, directing the nozzle into the drain before he opened fire—"SSSSSSSHHHHH!"

He was gone as abruptly as he appeared, and then I noticed the smell wafting out of the bathroom, which made me wonder-- was the long-banned (in the USA, anyhow) pesticide DDT still legal in Mexico?

"Everything is legal in Mexico," Chris said when he and Donna returned, and Donna wondered, while sniffing the air, if they mopped the floor with the stuff.

We decided if a cockroach did make it four flights up that drainpipe, it would be the baddest *cucaracha* south of the Rio Grande! And then, sure enough, on the last day of our stay, one cornered Donna in the bathroom.

BEACH BLANKET BANDITO

All I knew about Mexican blankets was that I liked them and I wanted one. I hadn't priced them anywhere or even touched one, but with just a few days left I was getting *consumeritis*.

First, I bought little toys for my boys, Eli and Riley, who were back in Willits with their Mom. A spinning top, a "Frito Bandito" puppet, a little box that opens to a snake popping out. You know, educational toys. Then I bought some useful items: a hammock, a straw hat, and more over-the-counter penicillin, my *Tourista* Insurance Package (TIP).

I was sitting on the beach looking out at Banderas Bay for whales. I read somewhere that humpback whales migrate thousands of miles each winter for only one reason—to mate! As a single male, I totally understood, but I saw no breaching whales or even any flukes slapping the water. I guess they're still pretty tired from their long journey, or they haven't found the perfect mate yet. I could relate to that too.

I also heard from a tourist that this beach was named *Playa de los Muertos,* which means Beach of the Murders. Long before this place became a tourist trap, some say a "pirate" murdered some locals, and the name stuck. The city attempted to change the name to *Playa del Sol—Sunny Beach*—but it didn't stick. This is the beach where hip bilingual tourists mingle with tourist-friendly locals. A lot of tanned skin, skimpy bikinis, volleyball, and loud music. A fun place to hang out.

I noticed a tanned *gringo* dickering with a native vendor over a stack of blankets. He turned out to be from Australia, and was quite pleased with himself for paying a trifling 2,000 pesos. "You couldn't buy one in the store this cheap, *mite,* that's less than ten dollars American money."

He convinced me, so I followed the vendor, but suddenly a second blanket vendor appeared, and I made the mistake of acknowledging his wares. The next thing I knew he had two blankets spread out on the sand, saying "Which one you like, *Senor?*"

"*Quantos pesos?*" I queried.

"Five thousand pesos," he shot back.

"No, no, *mucho mas, mucho mas.*" I shook my head and walked away.

"Okay, my friend," he called me back, "How much you give me?"

"Two thousand pesos," I winced with guilt for offering so little for his beautiful blanket.

He patiently disregarded my insult, and said, "Thirty-five hundred pesos."

"No, gracias Senor," and as I turned to walk away I heard, "Three thousand pesos, amigo."

I tried to tell him the Aussie paid two thousand from one of his competitors, but he didn't seem to understand, and when I turned to the Aussie for support, he said, "Don't bring me into this, mite."

The vendor's next ploy was to give up. He shrugged his shoulders in defeat, sighed, and said softly, "Okay, my friend, twenty-five hundred pesos." I decided I was still getting a great deal, I mean, where else can I get a fine blanket like this for $11.35?

As my new Aussie mite and I strolled down the beach, my new blanket draped over my shoulder, I thought, what's a measly five hundred pesos anyhow. What the heck, the vendor probably has several mouths to feed. Then the Aussie laughed and says, "I thought the red one you picked out was the ugliest of the stack. I liked the green one."

We left the beach, heading toward the street, and in the middle of the first block was a store with a stack of blankets just like mine. I gave the Aussie a shrewd let's-just-see-how-much-we-saved look, and asked the young clerk how much: *"Quantos pesos, por favor?"*

He looked me straight in the eye and said, as if it were a question, "Two thousand pesos?"

Aussie turned away, chuckling, and quipped, "All is not lost, mite, maybe he'll trade you that nice green one for your ugly red one. Hahaha"

A third tourist who happened to witness the conversation, volunteered, "You probably could get the kid down to fifteen hundred pesos."

The Perfect Tourista Insurance Package

I decided to keep a daily log on this trip, just in case I had a fit of inspiration, but as with most of my past travel logs, entries got shorter and shorter, and soon fizzled out altogether. With this in mind, the following entry was my first day, followed by my somewhat nostalgic last day.

Tuesday, February 5

Ah, our first day in paradise. Chris went out for a run, only to return nauseous. A touch of *tourista?* I told him to take some of my penicillin. Won't penicillin kill off any and all bacteria? My theory is that I can take chances while on the *wonder drug* I wouldn't normally take. Drink the water right out of the tap? Sure! Fruit straight from the shelf and into my mouth? No *problema.*

Yes, I believe I have discovered the secret tourists have sought for centuries! I have once and for all put Montezuma's infamous revenge to rest. And it was so obvious!

The only problem is my prescription runs out Saturday. What will happen then? Can I purchase the drug here without a prescription? Donna thinks I'll be even more susceptible when I stop my dosage. As it turned out, I bought some over-the-counter for less than half of what I paid in the USA!

Now that I was feeling better I decided it was time to find a good cup of coffee. I pictured a quaint neighborhood café with fresh roasted beans picked from the nearby hills, accompanied by a few slices of *pan dulce* (sweet bread).

I found what seemed to be the perfect place. No sign out front, only a few locals inside, dipping tortillas in soup. Dust floating in from the continuous taxi traffic outside the open doors and windows. This place was so authentic it didn't even have a menu. In fact, it was so low-key, for a moment I thought I was sitting in someone's dining room. But then this sweet *mamacita* appeared to take my order. They didn't have sweet bread so I had to settle for tortillas.

After 10 or 15 minutes, the time I imagined it took to grind the selected beans and brew that perfect cup, she appeared with a chipped cup full of warm water, a spoon, and a small jar of Nescafe crystals.

What!!! *Café instantáneo!!* They must have seen that stupid TV commercial of the guy whispering from the kitchen of some fancy Hollywood restaurant about to substitute Folger's crystals for the "fine coffee they usually serve."

Turns out that's what you get anywhere down here, no matter how fancy the restaurant. The worst part is I started enjoying my cup of Nescafe every morning, doctored up with milk and sugar, of course. It even crossed my mind that two spoonfuls of Nescafe every morning may kill its own share of bacteria, which makes Nescafe and penicillin the perfect Tourista Insurance Package!

Our Last Day February 14

Our last full day in paradise leaves us in a contemplative mood. Yesterday we joked about doing everything the last day—cram it all in: Parasailing, the bull fights, the boat trip to *Yelapa*...but here we sit reading and writing and mulling over what we did and didn't do.

Chris and Donna laughed over the fact that Star, a beautiful divorcee from Santa Fe, had been in the unit below us all alone for over a week, but I just met her yesterday. Haha.

Chris woke up feeling "Itchy to move on." If we weren't going back tomorrow, he would want to go "deeper into Mexico." We all agreed eight days here as a tourist was enough. We explored the back streets and found the better restaurants, satisfied our *consumeritis* at the *Mercado* (market). In fact, in my opinion, our *consumeritis* peaked out when Chris and Donna paid 5,000 pesos for an armadillo purse, with the head and feet still intact.

Any reluctance to leave may have to do with feeling more comfortable with the language, especially Donna, our fearless interpreter, who is now dreaming in Spanish, and has a hard time writing or even speaking without mixing the two languages. She feels her eight days here was worth "months in the classroom."

Of course, our friends back home will tell us we're not tan enough. In fact, preventing sunburn has been a higher priority. Any suffering we've seen here has not been by the natives begging in the streets (they actually make a pretty good living), but the red and white skinned time-conscious tourists who go from the airplane to the beach, eager for their money's worth of tropical sun.

Anyhow, I'm a more seasoned *tourista* than the one who walked through that lobby eight days ago and said, "Buenos Nachos."

Chris and Donna's laughter made me realize I had just greeted the hotel clerk with "Good chips."

Part-time Work for Full-time Pay

WHEN I GOT BACK FROM Mexico at the end of February I was told by my landlord's son that he and his partner were taking over the property to mill their redwood and store their poles, and needed to use my rental unit for an office for their new *Willits Redwood Company*.

So, I'm back in Willits without a job, soon to be without a place to live, and wouldn't get my teacher's retirement check until summer. I didn't actually retire, but quit. I got what you might call early burnout. Still, the district owed me about a grand per year that I had put into the kitty, and since I'd saved enough money to live on for a while, I wasn't worried. Plus, I did make fifty cents an inch writing a weekly column for The Willits News called *FootNotes*.

My column was mostly about running, which had become more and more popular, with more road races and marathons showing up in Northern California and across the country every year. I would go to run these races, usually with my two boys, and then write about them. When I was introduced to local folks, they usually responded with, "Oh, you're the runner," and then they'd tell me why they don't run.

The main reason I decided to remain in Willits was because of my boys, who were living with their mom in town in the place we bought back in 1978 with money she inherited when her grandma passed away two years earlier. The next year I built a two-story addition off the back so we'd all have a little more room, but in '81 I had an affair with a friend's 21-year-old daughter and that pretty much was the end of our ten-year relationship.

Yvonne and I had a good ten-year run, in fact, looking back makes me think that we should be able to choose the length of the marriage we want to serve, like the military. Let's say we could choose a five-year, ten-year, or twenty-five year term. Or the traditional "to death do us part." But does it really get much better after ten years? Of course, we could renew the wedding vows, but also feel free to walk away, take a break, see what else is out there. A win-win situation, and the best part is you wouldn't have to go through a nasty divorce. Just hang in there until your time is served. Then you're free.

My friend Neva said I could stay in the house her ex built on their 20-acre property before he decided to go his own way, plus she wouldn't charge me any rent if I just made it more livable. A live-in home improvement project with no pressure was just what I needed, and it was only five miles from town.

Another friend said he had some extra marijuana starts he'd give me. Although I never grew cannabis before, I had smoked on and off since that first time in Milwaukee back in 1967. I remember four of us sitting around a friend's living room floor passing a Mexican joint around and I stubbornly insisted I felt nothing. Then driving home, when the stop light went from green to red it was like the red was really bright!

"Wow!! Look how bright that red light is!" I awed, as if it was the brightest red light I'd ever seen. My fiancée Lois laughed and brought me out of my denial with, "You're stoned, Jimmy!"

MY ONE-HIT WONDER
Neva said I could grow ten plants, but not near the house, and she pointed to a ridge that was on the highest, most distant part of her property. The

good news was that ridge was high enough to get full sun almost all day, causing those plants to grow big and hearty.

The bad news was I broke my ankle a week or so after getting them in the ground, which made it really difficult to climb up that craggy hill, with or without my crutches, to tend to them. I was forced to crawl on my hands and knees, using leather gloves and knee pads, for six weeks to nurture those greedy monsters. But it was worth it, I got twelve pounds off ten plants, and the price of pot was going up. That year it hit $2000 a pound, and if you knew the right people it didn't take long to get rid of it.

To sum up for the record books, ten marijuana plants earned me more money than my last year of teaching in the public school system. Also, I should mention, in case the Feds are reading this, I paid taxes on the money, but called the work carpentry, since I wasn't getting paid for the carpentry I did on Neva's extra house, it somehow made sense to me at the time. What else made sense to me was how my friend who gave me the starts summed it up: "Growing pot is part-time work for full-time pay."

By the end of September I started harvesting. I wanted to test each of the plants separately to see what I had, so by mid-morning every day or so, when the sun came through the window to my cleaning station, I would take a dried bud from one of my ten plants and roll a joint. Then I would smoke it and just observe my reaction. Every high made me feel good, made me breath deep, move around, and unless I already went for a run that morning, made me want to do something physical.

One day I smoked some of my *kush*. Most of my plants were cannabis sativa, but this was cannabis *indica*. It looked different than the *sativa*, not as tall but thicker, the leaves wider and the buds coated with resin. It also had a more potent odor, what some later called "skunk weed." But maybe best of all was that it matured faster. This was especially important during the C.A.M.P. years (Campaign Against Marijuana Planting) with helicopters flying all around the county during harvest time.

I had only a few hits and the next thing I knew I was outside in a patch of sun, barefoot, and doing tai chi. I stood there breathing deeply, feeling centered and tuned in to everything around me. The squirrels were chattering, the birds were tweeting, and a western fence lizard was doing push-ups on a sunny rock, looking in my direction in a challenging manner.

That by far became my favorite of the ten. I shared it with a few people, but I didn't want to sell it. The sad part was my friend didn't have the seeds to that particular strain, so it was a one-hit wonder.

So how did I break my ankle? I wrote about it in one of my *FootNotes* columns. I broke it running the *Dipsea*, a footrace in Marin County from Mill Valley over Mt. Tamalpais to Stinson Beach. That race in '85 was the 75th running and it's still going strong.

(The following is an edited version of my 1985 *FootNotes* column from *The Willits News*)

The *Dipsea* is a handicap footrace that starts in downtown Mill Valley and winds up and up and up 671 stairs to Muir Woods, around the slopes of Mt. Tamalpais, and down to the finish line in Stinson Beach. The 75TH annual *Dipsea* was run last Sunday, making it the second oldest continuous footrace in the United States, behind only the Boston Marathon.

I've been wanting to run this 7.4-mile trail run since I joined the Tamalpa Runners last year after turning forty because they're the closest club with a competitive Masters Team, and I was told that if you haven't run the *Dipsea* you're a "running virgin."

To reduce the crowded conditions on the trail, the field is limited to 1,500 runners, and the age-handicap start gives older and younger runners up to a 20-minute head start. Being 40-years old, I had a 2-minute head start, which meant I had to pass nearly 700 runners on the narrow steps and trails to finish near the front and receive one of the thirty-five coveted black t-shirts.

Since the more people you have to pass on the single-file trail, the slower your time, this race is ideal for the fit older and younger runners who get to start before most of the crowd. One of the fittest older runners in the country is 45-year old Sal Vasquez, who won this year for the fourth straight time. Sal had a 4-minute head start, which meant he had his share of runners to pass, but still ran the fastest *scratch* time with a 49:56!

Perhaps the best way to describe this rugged, root-infested trail is to list some of the names along the way: Suicide Hill, Cardiac Hill, Steep Ravine, and Insult Hill, to a name a few.

According to the Marin Independent Journal, 85 runners suffered an assortment of strains, sprains, abrasions, and heat exhaustion. One runner was taken to Marin General Hospital for a "possible torn tendon." Actually, that runner sustained more than a torn tendon, he suffered "an avulsion of the right distal fibula." An avulsion is a ripping off, a tearing away. In laymen's terms, this runner broke his ankle.

He was charging down Insult Hill, trying to make up for lost time due to a wrong turn, when suddenly his ankle snapped and he flipped into a dry creek bed, rolled into a boulder, and without losing his place, jumped back on the trail and finished the race, hobbling like the Hunchback of Notre Dame.

It may seem crazy to run the last mile on a broken ankle, but this runner wasn't sure if it was broken, he just thought it was a bad sprain, and all he could think about was getting to the finish line and putting ice on it. He finished in 33rd place, earning one of the coveted 35 T-shirts, with a scratch time of 54:58.

He felt stupid and embarrassed and extremely sorry for himself. If you happen to see this runner in Willits, treat him as you would any other cripple on crutches. Don't ask him if he wants to go jogging—haha—he's a sensitive human being, just like some of you.

Sweet and Sour Pup

"HEY DAD, TELL US ABOUT the time you ate one of Tala's puppies," asked ten-year old Riley recently.

"Who told you about *that*?!" I demanded, although I knew.

"Mom and Sally were talking about it," Eli, my oldest boy, answered. They both seemed keen on getting my reaction, hearing my side of the story.

"Did you kill it and everything?" Riley wondered, wrinkling his nose in disgust.

"Hell no, I ate it while it was still alive, one leg at a time, and then the nose, like you'd eat an animal cracker."

They both laughed, partly because I was funny, and maybe more from the relief that perhaps the story wasn't true after all. Just when I thought I was off the hook, Eli added, almost sadly, "Mom said she'd never forgive you for that."

"Oh, is that right? And do you think I even give a shit what she or anyone else thinks!" I guess I got a little defensive.

"Yes, I did eat one of Tala's damned puppies, but she had a shitload of the little buggers and they were driving me nuts. Besides, you should understand that many countries consider dog meat a delicacy. It's a cultural thing, what one country might consider a rare treat, another won't feed to their...dog."

They looked at me, wondering if that was supposed to be funny, but I continued. "Did you ever eat fish eggs?"

"Ich!" Riley reacted at the thought, but Eli knew what I was getting at, and said quickly, "Caviar!"

"Right!" I answered, in typical school teacher fashion. "Caviar is a delicacy to the rich and ostentatious, but it's just fish eggs to us." And we all made a sour face.

"In India," I went on, "cows are sacred. People wouldn't think of hurting, let alone eating a cow, but in this country most people can't go a day without eating COW MEAT! HAM BURGER! T-BONE STEAK! CALF LIVER! COW TONGUE!"

I was on roll. "What do you think the Eskimos do when they can't catch any fish or kill any seals or polar bears? Huh? Do you think they suck snow cones? DOG MEAT!!!

In this country, we learn to love puppies and kitties and ponies and Bambis and all those cutesy-wootsy furry animals, but what do you think hungry people in China and Mexico and Korea eat?"

And we say it all together: "DOG MEAT!!!"

"Wouldn't you like to go to McDonald's and order a coke, French fries, and some Puppy McNuggets?"

They both laughed, and then Eli asked the obvious: "What does it taste like?"

"A cross between chicken and pork, I guess. My friend who cooked it added a lot of spices and stuff...hey, do you want the recipe?"

"Sure dad, mom would really like that." And we laughed again.

"Who cooked it?" Riley wondered.

"Ah...her name is Cynthia. She lives in Hawaii now. She was a friend who came up for a visit when we were living up on Shimmin's Ridge...back in the summer of '75. Look guys, I'd tell you the story, but you'd just be bored."

"Just tell us the good parts," Eli countered, both smiling eagerly with anticipation.

"No, I have to tell you the WHOLE story."

This was actually a bluff on my part because I really didn't want to tell them that I took a .22 rifle and shot a puppy in the head, then watched it convulse before shooting it again so it would stop shaking. I didn't want to explain what Cynthia was doing up there, yet I didn't feel like apologizing either. No, we didn't have any meat, but that's not why I did it. I don't know, it seemed like a real practical thing to do at the time. Here were thirteen little eight-week old, dinner-sized puppies running around, and I guess I complained a bit too much, so Cynthia finally asked if I ever had sweet and sour pup. It first struck me as funny, but I could see she was serious. "You kill it and I'll do the rest," I remember her saying.

Two thoughts came immediately to mind: 1) Could I kill it? and 2) What would Yvonne do when she found out?

Yvonne was the woman I lived with, and the mother of Eli and Riley, though Riley wasn't born yet. She had taken Eli to her grandmother's funeral in San Diego. After I dropped them off at the train depot, I went to visit some friends in Sausalito, and found myself sharing a bottle of cheap red wine with Cynthia Rabbit. Rabbit was just her nickname because she raised rabbits. She was another misplaced mid-westerner who had found a home in the close-knit floating community of Waldo Point. Tied up to her houseboat was a floating dock piled high with rabbit hutches. Cynthia loved, fed, traded, and butchered her rabbits, as anyone raising rabbits might do.

I was telling her about life up on the land, how I hurt my foot, and how hard it was getting around on one leg. It suddenly occurred to me that she might want to come up and visit. I would really appreciate some help and then I could bring her back next week when I returned to pick up Yvonne and Eli.

"Sure," she said, happy to go to the country for a while.

At that point, I hadn't really thought of Cynthia as someone I wanted to be romantically involved with, even for a week. I just liked her because she was fun to talk to, and maybe because she was also from Wisconsin. Whenever I get a little homesick, I find it helps to hang out with a Wisconsin native for a while.

How much of this story should I tell the kids? Is killing a puppy any worse than killing a bunny rabbit? Is spending a week with another woman while mom's away any better or worse than killing a puppy or a bunny? And why is their mother still so angry about an event that took place twelve years ago? Maybe it's the combination of killing her puppy and then sharing it with another woman over a bottle of cheap red wine?

As expected, they lost interest while I went into this long, boring introduction. Instead of telling them the good parts (i.e. their mom's reaction to the sex and murder), I told them about when I worked for the county in Laytonville, and how I got these terrible blisters on my feet that gave me blood poisoning, and how Yolanda freaked when she saw the red streaks going up my leg, and how she made me go to the hospital because, as she said, "I don't want to wake up next to a corpse."

They still had one ear tuned in to my monologue, still waiting for the "good parts." I explained how I had to drive fifteen miles to the closest hospital, and for the equivalent of a week's beer money, got a prescription for antibiotics just so Yvonne wouldn't have to "wake up next to a corpse."

I didn't tell them how much I enjoyed my week in the country with a different woman; a young, attractive woman, eager to try something new, and willing to do all the chores and even cook exotic meals while I lounged around nursing a few blisters.

It wasn't until I had picked up Yvonne and Eli, done all our shopping, and were heading home that she finally asked how the animals were doing, and how big the puppies were. I had been anticipating these questions, of course, and figured she wouldn't even remember how many damned puppies there were -- twelve, thirteen, who gives a shit, right? No way did I intend to tell her I ate one of the little buggers. But hiding the fact that Cynthia had been up while she was gone would not be so easy. So, I just came out and told her that Cynthia was up for the week to help out.

Her reply was as expected: "Did you fuck her?"

It was a dumb question, I mean, a week alone in the country with a healthy, young female. If I said no, I'd be lying, but if I said yes, I'd be admitting my guilt. I had to change the subject, get her mind off sex, so like a real dummy, I said, "We ate one of Tala's puppies."

At this point in our conversation we had reached the worst stretch of our rutted logger-road driveway; the place where the road narrows at the same time you have to negotiate an uphill, hairpin turn on loose gravel.

Her sense of outrage was much finer honed than her sense of humor, or for that matter, her sense of safety, causing a typically irrational response -- she started hitting me in the face.

So, I'm trying to drive with my left hand and defending my face with my right. Everything past the hood is a blur because my glasses flew off with her first hit, and yet for some reason I'm laughing.

While she's yelling and crying and flailing her hands in my face, I'm trying to keep the fucking car on the road, and Eli's sitting behind us in his car seat eating a banana, wondering what the hell is going on? Why is mom so pissed off? Why is dad laughing? Do other adults act like this? Oh well, we'll be home soon and everything will be all right again.

But everything wasn't all right again and never would be. I don't know why I bothered to confess, since I didn't really think she'd ever find out. Hell, she didn't even want to know. Why did I tell her?

We said little to each other besides perfunctory routine stuff for a few days. She would cry sometimes just looking at Tala or one of her puppies. She was extremely sensitive. Apparently losing her grandmother and then coming home to my little surprise was a bit much, and I truly regretted the whole affair.

Then one day we were sitting outside, warming up to each other again. I felt she was ready to forgive me, or at least let it go, as she was saying something nice to me for the first time in several days.

Then I noticed what looked like a small animal skin stretched out on the manzanita bush just over her right shoulder. Of course, I realized immediately what it was, and didn't want her to see it. That's all we needed, a little furry reminder of Cynthia's visit. But she noticed I had seen something over her shoulder and said, "What is it?"

"What is what?" I answered coolly.

She repositioned herself so that if she looked over her right shoulder she would be almost eye level with the puppy skin. "I just thought you saw something behind me," she answered, swiveling her head slightly.

I felt I had to do something quick, so I got up and fell down, as if I had twisted my ankle. "Shit!" I cried.

"You okay?" she moved toward me.

"Yeah, I tweaked my ankle a little bit. Help me over to the deck, would you?" I winced slightly as I got up, and she took my arm.

In the safety of the deck I told her my ankle felt better, but she forgot her glass of water, and before I could think of what to do or say, she was half-way to the manzanita bush to retrieve her drink.

I heard a sharp whimper, as if she got the wind knocked out of her, and as she strode past me into the house she snarled, "Just get rid it of it!"

I remember walking down the meadow with this puppy skin on a stick. As I approached the puppy pen, a dozen of the survivors came running over wagging their tails. I held the dangling skin above their heads until one of the friskier ones snagged it, and a few more sank their teeth into it, snarling playfully, pulling it back and forth.

Watching these little critters play tug-of-war with what was left of their dead sibling made me laugh. "It's a dog-eat-dog world," I told them, and added, "I wonder which one of us is next?"

Rudy behind me at my desk holding a *joint* that I didn't see until after his friend took the photo. He showed me it was made of pencil shavings.

Birth Control--Free Zone

HER NAME WAS JOLENE AND she had been a student of mine when I taught at the local continuation high school. She dropped out of the regular high school at fifteen, pregnant with her first child, then came to East Valley to get her diploma.

The atmosphere at East Valley was more relaxed than at the regular high school. We had a 10-1 student-teacher ratio, which gave us more individual one-on-one time with the students. They earned credits by fulfilling "contracts", and when they earned enough credits to graduate, we agreed on a date, had a modest ceremony, and they were gone.

Jolene was skinny and cute with big vulnerable brown eyes, a come-hither smile, and long, chalky-white legs. Maybe it was her down-home sense of humor that attracted me to her, or the way she moved her hands when she talked, as if marionettes dangled from her fingers. I don't know anymore, but it was always fun when she showed up.

She attended sporadically and eventually dropped out, married some local loser ten years older and had another baby. The marriage didn't last, he soon went his own way, and she came back to school, this time to study for the GED. She didn't last much longer the second time, and continued her existence in her family-operated trailer park.

I saw her a few times since then. Once bowling, my first time bowling in years. Boy she looked good, even with one of her front teeth missing. She said her husband was pissed off and "there was no dog to kick!"

Then I was running past the dam one day and she jumped out of a car and yelled, "Hi Jim!" She was with some guy so I didn't stop to chat, but the fantasy took hold. I couldn't get her out of my mind.

The next time was at Lake Mendocino. I was with my kids and she was with hers. We talked briefly, but again she was with some guy, who she flippantly wrote off, when I asked if he was her husband, "Him?" She made a face, "No, he's just some guy I live with." I raised my eyebrows and laughed, but she wasn't finished-- "I think of him as a date that never went home."

We returned to our respective blankets, but kept glancing at each other. At one point, she was rubbing suntan lotion on his back and smiling at me. Her smile sent a chill down my spine, and embarrassed me, as if the chill was visible, I turned away. A friend sitting with me said, "Cute, who is she?"

"An ex-student of mine," I told him.

"Well, in case you haven't noticed, your ex-student is flirting with you."

"You think so?" I asked, surprised at how obvious it was.

"Yes, and you're hot for her too!" We both laughed.

Since I couldn't shake her out of my consciousness, I decided to visit her. She had said she lived in a trailer park just north of town, so I cruised through the Little Lake Trailer Park looking for her green Chevy Nova, but I didn't see it. Her name wasn't in the telephone book, and since she was a welfare mother, I couldn't call her at work.

I gave up my half-hearted search, figuring Little Lake was a small town and I'd eventually run into her on the street or at Safeway. Besides, she was too young for me. What was I trying to prove? I didn't need an aging Lolita with two kids.

One night a friend suggested we drive down to the local bar for a beer. We were both lonely for female companionship, as neither of us had touched a non-platonic woman in weeks...okay, months. Anyway, I was telling him about Jolene, my ex-student fantasy.

"Is she twenty-one?" he asked.

"She must be." I calculated aloud, "She has a six-year-old daughter that she had when she was fifteen."

"If she's twenty-one," he said, pausing slowly for effect, "She's old enough."

Just then who walks through the door? Big smile on her face. Sits down on the bar stool next time mine and pulls out her I.D.

"I'm twenty-one," she announces. "My birthday's today."

I lean over and look at her I.D. "Sure enough," I say, "Give her a drink." And although she grew up in Little Lake Valley, this is her first time in a bar.

"I don't drink," she admits, before ordering some sweet alcoholic concoction. "But this is a special occasion."

She is only going to have one drink, but after I buy one, she buys one, and her sister buys one, she becomes glued to her bar stool.

"I better go cuz I don't like leaving my kids too long at the sitters," she says with conviction.

I know it's now or never. I have to figure out how to get a hold of her. "How can I contact you if I need to?" I ask lamely, as if something really important is going to come up and I'll have to discuss it with her.

"Got a pencil and paper?" she asks cheerfully, as if to say, "I thought you'd never ask."

"Just tell me," I say, confidently.

"2768" she replies, loud enough for the whole bar to hear. I repeat it and store it.

Another ex-student, Bob, who has been talking to us and quite obviously has his eye on her too, seems to take a mental note of her number. I'm getting jealous already and I haven't even asked her out yet! I direct the conversation to him to get his mind off her number. "So Bob, what have you been doing since you got out of the Navy?"

"Been working at the mill," he says.

"Pulling green chain?" I guessed.

"Yeah, I'd like to quit, but I bought a new Camaro and I got payments up the wazoo!"

"That's tough." I try to sound sympathetic.

A few drinks later she slides slowly off her bar stool, as if the floor had been lowered, and walks carefully to the lady's room.

Just before she leaves she asks me, "What's my number?"

"2768," I quickly rattle off, then look at Bob to see if he heard it. We were suddenly back in class and Bob was caught daydreaming again. Jolene and I look from Bob's blank face back to each other, and she smiles: "Good, now don't forget to call me."

And she's gone.

I turn a smug smile to my friend, who I ignored all this time. He just shakes his head in amazement and says: "Cosmic!"

Yes, I was twice her age, but it seemed to bother me more than it did her. I would stop over at her trailer and we would talk about any trivial bullshit. She would eventually put her kids to bed and we would make out.

But most nights before getting to Jolene, I had to endure her sister and her sister's boyfriend, who lived in the trailer next door. We would sit in the kitchen under the bare lightbulb and banter back and forth. Jolene's sister would urge her boyfriend to tell dirty jokes, then she'd steal the punchline and laugh too loud. She was full of gossip and sexual innuendos. I got the feeling she didn't approve of me "balling" (her word) her little sister.

Through these long, boring visits Jolene would hardly talk except to react to one of her sister's many embarrassing family secrets. I was willing to humor them only because when they finally left I'd be alone with Jolene. It was lust pure and simple.

What bothered me about Jolene was her I'll-be-in-a-trailer-park-all-my-life-attitude. "I've lived in trailer parks my whole life," she once said, proudly, "and I will continue to live in trailers. I'm even buying this one right now on the installment plan."

But she was just what I wanted, available whenever I got the urge, and best of all, no commitment. Hell, she was used to on-again, off-again relationships with guys like me.

It was the perfect set-up and so easy. Yet, I found myself trying to change her. I wanted her to stop smoking, eat better food (she bought Wonder Bread and Frosted Flakes), go outside in the sunshine once in a while and get some exercise! Aspire to something more than welfare and trailer parks, for *chrissake*! I wanted to change her, even though I should have known it was impossible.

Three things happened that finally ended this hot set-up. The first was her ex-husband Floyd. He was arrested for attempted robbery. He tried robbing the Bank of America after hours. He had thrown a brick through a large plate glass window and was found prying open an empty cash drawer. The story made the front page of the *Little Lake Ledger*, between the Mayor's Message and an article announcing the closing of the Little Lake Library.

His lame-brained scheme was to get caught to "help" Jolene. He thought she would somehow be taken care of if he were sent to prison. She told him if he really wanted to help her he should have killed himself. Floyd's pathetic ignorance and her cold attitude was very unsettling to me.

The second thing that turned me off was she thought she was pregnant. Not by me, but by some guy she went off with on a whim. A one-night fling in the back seat of his new Camaro. She didn't tell me this, her sister did. Her sister said Jolene thought the guy was cute and "she especially likes new Camaros." Jolene blushed.

My question was, "Why not have an abortion?" As she was trying to explain to me why her church was against abortion, my mind was wondering who I had talked to recently with "big wazoo payments" on a new Camaro?

"I thought you were taking the pill!" I demanded, wondering if she had lied to me.

"I forgot." She said simply.

"What is this area, a Birth Control--Free Zone!?" I blurted, referring to the recent campaign to make Little Lake Valley a *Nuclear Free Zone*. I had to explain that this was a play on words, ha ha, but no one laughed.

That's when I discovered the third thing that turned me off about this whole affair. She went to church. Her whole family went to church. Besides being against abortion, the church was against the *Nuclear Free Zone* Initiative because many in the church community worked at Dredco

Hydraulics and Macromorph Manufacturing. The initiative, which eventually failed, would have made these companies lose contracts that in turn would have resulted in layoffs.

She tried explaining why she believed in God, and why she goes to church every Sunday. "Why not?" she reasoned. "It can't hurt. If there is a God I'll go to heaven, and if there isn't, what the hell, I only invested one hour a week."

She seemed to think that sounded pretty rational, as if it were really well thought out, a truth so pure and simple it was miraculously overlooked by the great theologians and philosophers of recorded history.

I chuckled, shook my head, and started to squirm. The bare light bulb suddenly was too bright. Her sister and sister's boyfriend looked uneasy. The kitchen was too small for all of us. I looked down at the worn-out linoleum, littered with food crumbs. I noticed just the hint of cellulite on Jolene's right thigh.

I had to get the fuck out of there. I stood up and moved toward the door, mumbling something about being tired, gotta go, but stopped briefly at the door to say goodnight to Jolene.

Did she know why I was leaving? Did she know I wasn't coming back? Did she know how sexy she looked suspended in the half-light of the kitchen doorway?

Postscript: *Most names used in this flashback are made up, but most of the story is true.*

Le Tour de Clear-cut 1991

FROM MY DECK I SEE miles and miles of trees, mostly redwoods, and over the treetops out on the horizon sits the Pacific Ocean. On a clear night I see the lights of Fort Bragg, a coastal town about 17 miles west, as the crow flies. Or if you take Sherwood Road (the old Stagecoach Road) it's about 35, and 45 miles if you go into Willits and take Highway 20.

First time visitors stand on my deck and tell me I've got a million-dollar view, but I like to point out the large brown areas, the clear-cuts that appeared within the last year. I drove over the road in my old Willys Jeep about fifteen years ago, and still remember how thick the woods were, how damp and cool it was for the middle of a typical 90-degree summer day. Redwood forests are a haven in the summer because they soak up the coastal fog, and actually make the earth under them wet with their own rain.

I had been wanting to ride my mountain bike over the road for a long time, but couldn't get anyone to go with me. One Sunday morning in June I decided to just do it. I figured three hours by bike, two by truck. I left my driveway at 9:36 in the morning and planned to be in Fort Bragg by lunchtime. My girlfriend and her daughter followed 45 minutes later in my pickup and caught me about seven miles from the coast.

It took a while to peddle the first eight miles to Sherwood Peak, where *Earth First* recently buried a Pinto in the road to draw attention to the loggers who are methodically clearcutting this ridge, but from there it was downhill through a Louisiana-Pacific "tree farm," and about halfway to the coast, on Georgia-Pacific land, the cuts began.

The brown areas I could see from my deck were just the tip of the iceberg. Up close it was much worse than I imagined. I was riding through a war zone without any trees much bigger than ten inches in diameter. Even the ferns and redwoods right next to the road were recently cut, adding insult to injury, and making the once cool corridor now look like a set from *Road Warrior.*

What recently was an ancient redwood forest with huge puddles along the road that just 15 years ago required a four-wheel drive vehicle, now could be easily traversed with the family station wagon. Instead of worrying about getting lost in a primeval forest, I was worried about getting sunburned. It reminded me that the Sahara Desert was a forest at one time, too.

Yes, I've seen the lumber trucks going up and down Sherwood Road. I've seen tons of stockpiled logs in town, and I knew the cutting had been accelerated, but to see for myself that they've already clear-cut hundreds of acres within my view was shocking. This destruction was going on in my own backyard and who was doing anything to stop it? Who even knew about it?

Earth First was alone in their efforts to slow down the loggers by confronting them, as Anna Marie Stenberg did when she threw a logger's ax down the hill during the Caltrans cut on Highway 20. A ballsy thing to do, as is climbing a tree with a logger standing by with his chainsaw, or chaining yourself to logging equipment. Some believe extreme measures are called for to draw attention to this irreversible destruction.

Liberals say *Earth First* actions like this alienate people, and reinforce the image of radical hippie monkey-wrenchers, who smoke dope and spike trees. This is about as accurate as saying that timber workers really care about the environment, practice sustained yield forestry to ensure work for future generations, and spend their weekends planting trees with their families.

What about replanting trees? Whatever happened to sustained yield? Are loggers proud of their work? Do they stand back and look at the acres of tree stumps and piles of slash and pat themselves on their backs? Do they show their children the fine work they're doing? Are we supposed to respect these guys? Are we supposed to care if they lose their jobs? Didn't they know that they were destroying a temperate rainforest, and their own logging future in Northern California? They don't really think the forest will grow back, do they? It seems to me that most loggers don't give a damn about future generations or they wouldn't make the mess they're making. If they are the new endangered species, as their bumper stickers say, so be it! And from what I've seen of their work, the sooner the better!

Some say I shouldn't blame the loggers, it's the corporations. I'm supposed to believe that timber workers must do whatever some millionaire corporate executive says in order to pay their mortgages and feed their families? Are timber workers saying they are too stupid to be retrained? If the guy in the suit tells them to cut down every tree in the county, will they do it?

After riding the last 10-12 miles through the clear cuts in all directions, I approached the blacktop outskirts of Fort Bragg. As I came swooshing down into town what I noticed most were stacks and stacks of firewood everywhere, and smoke rising from chimneys, as the fog was slowly burning off. A big lot on the left with every tree cut down had a sign that read: "Future home of Grace Trinity Church." Another lot with a new home being built on it had only recently downed trees on it. Why didn't they leave a few trees, I wondered?

I whizzed by a sign nailed to a fence (they couldn't find a tree) that read, "We support the timber industry." I wondered if they had taken a drive up

Sherwood Road anytime in the last few years so they could see for themselves what a great job the timber industry was doing.

When I told Judi Bari about my ride she told me *Earth First* was planning an *Ecotopia Bike Ride* on Highway 20 in August. I felt they should abandon Highway 20 because of the traffic and having to deal with Caltrans. I suggested they do it on Sherwood Road and call it *Le Tour de Clear-cut.*

I figured the best way to stop the cutting would be to focus attention on the area you could see. I didn't want *Earth Firsters* on bikes, confronting loggers in pickup trucks. I didn't want any one to get hurt, especially me. I wanted mountain bike riders to come and see for themselves what was happening, so they could spread the word.

Judi liked the idea of the Sherwood Road ride, but was set with her local organizers to do the Highway 20 ride on Saturday, August 17, and though they did add the Sherwood Road ride on Sunday, they were both to be called the *Ecotopia Bike Ride.* I was disappointed because I thought my idea of calling it *Le Tour de Clear-cut* was catchy. Made me wonder if they had ever heard of the *Tour de France.*

The Saturday ride attracted over 200 bicyclists. Many rode from town up to *Three Chop Ridge*, joining others who had their bikes trucked from town or base camp. People waited there for what was supposed to be a noon start for the 9-mile downhill run to Chamberlin Creek Conservation Camp, where Earth First! organizers had set up Ecotopia banners, free food was to be served, and speakers, including Mendocino County Supervisor Norman de Vall, who at one point chastised "political" people who were invited but didn't come.

Tired of waiting for someone to tell us to go, we took off just before 12:30 and spun down the newly blacktopped road doing speeds up to 50 mph. Not me, but someone on a racing bike bragged that he hit fifty.

There were some scary moments as a few of these curves are pretty radical and I was especially careful at the one where I had a head-on accident last April.

I was heading to Fort Bragg for the *Sunset Run* with 12-year old Riley and 6-year old Joanie in the back seat, and Susan riding shotgun, in my Toyota Corolla. Suddenly a white BMW came sliding around the turn and there was nothing to do but brace ourselves. Fortunately, we were all wearing seatbelts and nobody was hurt. But on a bike I'd be lucky to survive even if I was wearing a helmet.

There were no mishaps on Saturday and at the end of the ride there was plenty of food, thanks to Seeds of Peace, and more than enough Ben & Jerry's ice cream. Some people even took a ride back up and did it again. Others listened to politicians, poets, and singers, including Judi Bari on her fiddle, with Darryl Cherney on guitar.

Sunday Morning *Tour de Clear-cut*

The following morning, I left home on my *Rock Hopper* for the short ride over to 3rd Gate to meet with other bikers for the 30-mile ride to Fort Bragg. My girlfriend warned me to be careful and not to lead, as you never know what might be around the next bend, but I scoffed at her paranoid precaution, assuring her that an old fart like me wouldn't be able to keep up with these young bikers. But she knows my history. She knows I'm competitive and dangerous and pushing fifty. She's heard the story about how I snapped my ankle while running down Insult Hill during the 1985 *Dipsea* footrace over Mt. Tamalpais and down to Stinson Beach. How I finished the last mile hobbling so pathetically that my 12-year-old son, Eli, said he thought I had "to shit real bad," to which I answered, "I wish!"

Between 8:30 and 9:30 a.m. some 60 bikers rolled out Sherwood Road for what I like to call the first annual *Tour de Clear-cut*. Riders were struck by the beauty of the Sherwood Valley. We peddled past the historic *Octagon*

House and up to our first stop at Sherwood Peak, the tallest peak in the area at 3,300 feet, and where *Earth Firsters* buried the Pinto.

Our next stop was the spring to fill our water bottles, less than a mile further downhill. The fact that we dropped from about 3,000 feet to sea level meant of course that there was a lot of fast downhill. We made several stops along the way, almost too many stops, and we were anxious to get on with it. We were talking and checking mile markers, by no means racing, though a few of us agreed it would be a fun race. I see it as a race in stages, with one required five or ten-minute stop just past the halfway mark over-looking the vista of clear-cuts, with a requirement to share your thoughts to a video camera.

Organizer Dave Beebe, who caught up to us about halfway in a flatbed truck carrying water and supplies, sees this as an educational trek, as well as a physical challenge. He was putting up signs showing points of interest such as one stop where we examined the stump of an old growth tree that had every sucker around it cut, leaving nothing. And this was right next to the road. It was like you could look around and count the redwood trees on the fingers of one hand. And they were "pecker polls." Remember, this was a first, then a second-growth redwood forest, and these cuts were legal cuts. Someone wondered out loud if this could ever be a Redwood forest again.

We stopped again at a fork in the road with about 12 miles to go, one road leading down past a Georgia-Pacific gate and vistas of clear-cuts to the southeast, and the other road down a narrow, twisty part of the main road where Dave took the flatbed to the next aid station. We waited until the dust settled and without giving it much thought, I jumped on my bike and headed down the hill first, surprised at how suddenly steep and narrow the road became.

I was standing on the pedals, zigzagging down the mountain approaching a blind curve, when just about the time I realized I was going too fast to safely negotiate the curve, a blue Ford pickup appeared. I had a few seconds to respond, but in that time I knew I couldn't turn my wheel to avoid him without going down, and hitting his steel reinforced grill was going to hurt! My main concern was keeping my head up, as I was NOT wearing a helmet. Funny thing, we had just been talking about helmets at the last stop and I said I kind of wished I'd worn mine.

I did brake slightly, but dirt roads ain't blacktop, and I took the hit with my left foot, the bike shifter digging a long, punishing groove into my calf. I was on the ground for only a moment before jumping up to shake it off, trying to deny that I was hurt, but my calf in those few seconds swelled to twice its normal size, and wasn't done yet. I knew I needed some ice and the sooner the better.

The driver got out and asked if I was alright. "No. I'm hurt," I said, pointing to my swelling leg. Do you have any ice?" He said no, so I jumped back on my bike and headed down the hill to the next aid station where I knew Dave had ice, holding my injured, throbbing leg away from the pedal.

Meanwhile the driver of the truck, Wilbur P. James of Fort Bragg, stayed right there with his doors open having to deal with the anger of other bikers, some thinking he ran into me on purpose. One guy gave him a hard time and was cited by Deputy Jeff Courtney for interfering with an officer. Evidently, he refused to give his name because he didn't want to say it aloud for fear of retaliation from the two men in the pickup.

The same officer soon drove down the hill to questioned me, with both drivers present, and at least two video cameras rolling. I admitted that I was out of control, but I didn't mention that I thought the driver could have stopped sooner. Funny thing is, Dave Beebe had just stopped and warned him to be careful because bikers were coming down the hill. Yet he had to keep coming. And why was he even there to begin with? Oh, what the hell? It's a free country and this is a county road. We were just in the wrong place at the wrong time.

Yet, Judi Bari says that this driver and his buddy are the same guys who heckled her at a rally two weeks earlier, and they even warned her that *Earth First* should not do the Sherwood Road ride, or "there's going to be an accident." She said it's not an accident when someone announces it two weeks before it happens. Maybe Judi should have warned me? I never heard this threat until I read it in the next day's newspaper.

The next day on local radio stations KZYX and KMUD, I was quoted as saying these guys were "up to no good." I really said that "someone said that they were up to no good," meaning they were not there as part of anyone's support crew. Wilbur wore a T-shirt that said "Loggers are the new endangered species," and Cecil, his buddy riding shotgun, wore a hat that said "I hate Iraq." They were friendly to me and seemed relieved that I wasn't hurt any worse, but also somewhat intimidating

If I only had a few scrapes and bruises I could forget about it, but my calf is worse today, three days later, and I don't heal quickly anymore. Rich Reardon of Sacramento, who was right behind me and saw everything, was amazed that I got off without major injury. He told me, as people always do when I get sick or have an accident, that I'm lucky, it could have been worse. I believe it, I really do, but it could have been much better, too. Next year, just to make sure, I'm going to let Rich or one of those other young guys lead. I swear!

POSTSCRIPT: *I was not an Earth Firster, but I met Judi Bari several months after the bombing when I was hired to fix up the cabin she would be living in during her recovery. She moved in while I was building an addition off the front, including a bathroom, with a secret cubbyhole to hide her pot.*

Mike Sweeney, her ex-husband, would drop their two daughters off and pick them up, never smiling and always seemed angry. I asked her once, "What's he so pissed off about?" She said he was mad "because the bomb didn't kill me."

For those who don't know, Judi and her friend Darryl Cherney left the Earth First office in Ukiah for a rally in Oakland in May of 1990. While driving in Oakland, a bomb that someone put under her driver seat, probably while parked at the Earth First office in Ukiah, exploded.

Bruce Anderson, editor of the *Anderson Valley Advertiser*, has been following the case and writing about it since it happened. Now, twenty years after her death from cancer in 1997, he summed it up as follows:

"Judi Bari was a regionally prominent Earth Firster who was nearly killed by a 1990 car bomb. Bari herself, and her partisans, blamed a leftwing checklist of preferred villains—timber corporations; the FBI; Christian fanatics; men generally. The revolving cast of preferred suspects always excluded Bari's ex-husband, Mike Sweeney, a man with a long association with the bomb-throwing wing of the 60's left.

Post-bombing, Bari became something of a cult figure among lockstep "progressives" and their megaphones at KPFA, Democracy Now, and public "free speech" radio stations in Mendocino and Humboldt counties, where dissenting views on the case were not allowed.

Bari parlayed her alleged martyrdom at the hands of the mentioned forces into a winning federal lawsuit that claimed she'd been libeled by the FBI and Oakland Police Department, whose representatives had prematurely claimed Bari had been knowingly carrying the bomb that nearly killed her.

Several million dollars was won by Bari and Cherney in their lawsuit, and the FBI announced that they'd closed their investigation "because no one will talk to us." The case remains unsolved, and is referred to now as a "mystery," while the only mystery is why the biggest elephant in the room, her ex-husband, got a free pass from law enforcement.

The only honest investigation was done by Steve Talbot, formerly the producer of PBS's *Frontline* series. Talbot's documentary for

KQED is called, *Who Bombed Judi Bari*. Talbot, speaking live on KQED's "This Week in California" news show, said that Bari told him she was certain her ex was responsible. How many ex-husbands could not only get away with bombing their ex-wives but never even be considered a suspect?"

Neal Beckman with devil horn tatoos.

The Walmart Shootout March 7, 2003

I FIRST HEARD ABOUT THE Walmart shootout on the morning news, then read about it in the local newspapers. An ex-con with a long history of violence triggered a parking lot shootout at Ukiah's Walmart Friday night that left one police officer wounded, a security guard stabbed, and the shooter dead.

Police said Neal Allen Beckman, 35, confronted Ukiah Police Sergeant Marcus Young Friday night after Beckman's girlfriend was arrested for shoplifting. As officer Young and the girlfriend sat in Young's patrol car, Beckman approached with his hands in his coat pockets. Young ordered him to take his hands out of his pockets, which he did, but in one hand he had a big knife and the other a .38 Smith and Wesson.

Beckman continued to walk toward Young, firing five rounds at point blank range, hitting Young in the cheek, neck, shoulder and hand. Young was also hit in the chest, but his bulletproof vest no doubt saved his life.

The real hero of the day was 17-year-old police cadet Julian Covella, a Ukiah High School junior who ran from cover and out into the open to come to Young's aid. Young, bleeding profusely while kneeling help-lessly on the parking lot pavement, couldn't draw his gun from the holster because one of the bullets paralyzed his shooting hand. Covella pulled the gun out of Young's holster and placed it in his other hand.

Officer Young then fired three or four shots toward Beckman, who was trying to remove the loaded shotgun locked in Young's patrol car rack.

Meanwhile, Beckman's girlfriend is handcuffed in the backseat screaming bloody murder.

"Neal was hit in the head with one of the first shots," she explained, "But he wasn't dead, just shaking convulsively. He was about a foot from me. There was blood everywhere, but he still wasn't dead."

When I first heard the name Neal Beckman it rang a bell, taking me back some twenty years to my teaching days in the Willits Unified School District. *Beckman, Neal Beckman,* I kept saying to myself. I knew he had been a student of mine, but I couldn't picture him, so I did the math in my head. If he was 35, then twenty years ago he was 15, so that was 1983 when I taught at San Hedrin, the continuation high school.

Needless to say, teaching and residing in a small town means you see your students and ex-students quite often, and occasionally read their exploits in *The Willits News.* None that I recall got scholarships to Stanford or Harvard, but over the years I've recognized a few names in the weekly *Police Log.* There was a photo of him in the newspaper, but twenty years can change one's appearance. The photo showed a balding guy covered in tatoos. His most prominent tats were the devil horns on his forehead.

I decided to call my old friend Ed Schuman, who taught both at the high school and with me at San Hedrin. I asked him if we had a Neal Beckman at San Hedrin, and he chuckled, "Yeah, you took his gun away."

Then it all came back to me. It was 1983, out on the playground. Besides teaching English and a journalism class, where we put out *The San Hedrin High Times,* I taught PE. We usually played volleyball, basketball, or kicked the hacky-sack around. I even had a running class for a while.

Anyhow, one day Beckman, a young-looking 15-year old with long blond hair, barely over five feet tall, showed up at the end of PE class. I acknowledged him and he walked up to me with a smile and pulled a pistol out of his jacket. Not in a menacing manner, but more like he was proud of it and wanted to share this fun show-and-tell toy with his teacher.

I said, "Neal, you can't bring a gun to school! Let me see that," and he gladly handed it over to me. I'm not a gun guy, so I don't recall what kind it was other than a decent-sized pistol. I asked him if it was loaded, and he smiled, as if to say, 'Duh, I don't carry a gun if it's not loaded.'

I told him I'd have to keep it until after school, then I would give it back. He agreed. (Just for the record, I really wasn't planning to give it back, I just said that.) I consulted with the other teachers, and the next thing poor Beckman knew he was handcuffed and in the back of a Willits Police car. When the cops drove away, Beckman was said to have a big smile on his face.

Two years later I read that he and an accomplice knocked on the door of a local Willits resident, saying their car broke down and asked to use his phone. According to the victim's son-in-law, "they stabbed him four times in the back, and when he was on the ground they kicked every rib in his ribcage and beat him over the head with a cane."

During the trial the man died in the hospital, so they stopped the trial and were going to prosecute for murder, but he was just 17, so instead of trying him as an adult, they put him in a juvenile facility until he was 25.

"My wife and I kept going down to the parole board to stop him from getting out, and they did keep him until he was 25," the son-in-law explained in a 2003 interview in *The Ukiah Daily Journal,* "but then they said, 'Well, we kept him as long as we can.'"

The son-in-law added, "I'm glad they got him, though the whole thing could have been avoided if they had just done their job 18 years ago."

Even though Beckman was in and out of the slammer a few times in his last ten years, I didn't hear about him again until the Wal-Mart shootout.

POSTSCRIPT: *If you can't imagine what it would be like to have your 18-year-old daughter bring home a 35-year-old ex-con boyfriend with devil horn tats on his forehead and a .38 in his pocket, I recommend reading Monica's Walk on the Wild Side, an article by Bruce Anderson, editor of the weekly* **Anderson Valley Advertiser,** *in his and Mark Scaramella's 2003 book,* **Mendocino Noir, a Collection of Crimes Large and Small.**

Brian Murphy Takes A Hike Dec. 2007

I WAS HANGING OUT IN my Waikiki condo watching the evening news when the top story was about a hiker lost on Mauna Kea. Michigan resident Brian Murphy, age 67, left the Visitor Center at the 9,000-foot level to hike up the Humu'ula Trail toward the 13,796-foot peak, wearing only light clothing, prompting the ranger on duty to warn him of an incoming storm and high winds.

Murphy left anyhow, and two hours later it snowed, driven by 70 mph winds. When the Park closed that evening, Murphy's car was still in the Visitor Center parking lot. The next morning Park Rangers, Big Island Firefighters, a canine team, and even the Coast Guard searched for the missing hiker through a foot of new snow in blizzard-like conditions. They found no trace of Murphy.

I had told my wife I knew a guy from Wisconsin named Brian Murphy. He was my teammate on the UW-Milwaukee track team back in '65 to '67. I agreed there are a lot of Brian Murphys out there, just like there are a lot of John Smiths and Joe Blows, and I had to admit the bald-headed guy in the TV photo didn't quite look like the Brian Murphy I remembered. Of course, that was 40 years ago. Who looks like they did 40 years ago?

Then the following day I caught the news again, they had a photo of Murphy playing with one of his grandchildren.

"That's him," I told her. I was sure this time.

For the next few days I thought a lot about Brian Murphy. I remembered how cocky he was. I had never met anyone that self-confident before, or since, who could actually back it up! He had spent four years in the Marines and seemed to know everything, all you had to do was ask him. He became my self-appointed mentor, and I would listen to him because, well, because he didn't really want to listen to me.

His main event was the decathlon, the ten events that require strength, speed, *and* endurance. Although I tried the decathlon too, I was mostly a middle-distance runner and a pole vaulter. He was better than me in nearly every event, and reminded me at every turn, but he also helped me and gave me good advice. He also had the obvious advantage of being bigger, stronger, and a step faster than me. I could beat him in the 400, sometimes, and the 1,500 meters, but the other eight events were his.

The event I hated losing to him the most was the pole vault. I had been a pole vaulter in high school before the fiberglass pole, when the pole was either steel or aluminum. In those days, you really had to work to get over the crossbar. Most pole vaulters before the fiberglass pole were wrestlers and gymnasts with well-developed upper bodies for pushing off from the pole. Between jumps I used to walk around on my hands like I saw the world record-holder Don Bragg do at meets.

Bragg's record was 15' 9" and he just could not get over 16 feet with his aluminum pole. Then a lanky guy named Brian Sternberg emerged with the new fiberglass pole and sprang over 16 feet for a new world record. Bragg immediately lodged a protest, but the A.A.U. let the record stand and Bragg retired and so did the old metal pole.

Murphy would charge down the runway with his 160-pound test fiberglass pole and really make that sucker bend, catapulting over the bar set at 14 feet and higher, whereas for me, weighing just 130 pounds, I got very little bend out of that pole, and the 14-foot mark eluded me.

He also started the Milwaukee Track Club, and put on meets every few weeks in the summer. During one Summer I entered in every event except the 35-pound weight throw. The event I hated most was the 3000-meter racewalk. My shin muscles got so tight I just broke into a jog after crossing the finish line in utter relief! It might have helped if I had practiced a little.

In the Summer of '66 I placed third in the Wisconsin State A.A.U. Decathlon. Murphy won of course, as he did every year, and got good enough to go to California for the '68 Olympic Trials, and eventually finish fourth behind the Bill Toomey, who went on to win Gold at the Mexico City Olympic Games.

Because Mexico City was at 7,200 feet elevation, the US needed a venue that would be approximately the same altitude. They found the highest spot in California at Echo Summit in South Lake Tahoe at, of all places, a middle school. Yeah, how many middle schools have held the Olympic Trials? Good question. I think the answer might be just that one.

As most people know your speed improves in the thin air, but endurance becomes a challenge, and it usually takes a few weeks to get acclimated. That's why many distance runners like to train at altitude to build up their lungs, then when they return to sea level it's easier to kick ass. It was no surprise that the Mexico City Olympic records were broken in every running event up to 1500 meters, including Bob Beaman's incredible 29' long jump.

Murphy's daughter and sister-in-law flew out from Michigan to help with the search, but after six days with still no sign of Murphy, they officially gave up.

His daughter was quoted as saying that Murphy was in "good physical condition, being an active skier and holder of numerous national records for the decathlon." She also added that he was knowledgeable about safety and survival skills. "I see him as a person who would not panic in this situation, even if hurt, he overcomes pain extremely well."

Well, I agree with most of that, but I don't believe Murphy broke any national records in the decathlon. UW-Milwaukee records, sure, and no doubt Wisconsin records, maybe even Michigan records, if he continued in the sport, but I never heard from him again, and my guess is his sister's claim was a bit of an exaggeration.

Anyhow, I waited two years to write this because I first wanted to go up to Mauna Kea myself and talk to the ranger who was the last person to talk to Murphy, and it took this long to finally make the trip.

Mauna Kea is not only the highest mountain in the Pacific, but the highest mountain in the world from the ocean floor--over 30,000 feet. But the real interesting thing about Mauna Kea is it's one of the best sites on earth for astronomical observations. There are thirteen observatories on the mountain, home to astronomers from fourteen nations. The most technologically advanced are the Keck Observatories, with the two Keck telescopes remotely controlled by technicians in Waimea and Hilo.

My wife and I eventually moved to the Big Island and bought a house in Waimea, a town of cowboys (*paniolos*) and astronomers, set at 2500 feet between the Kohala Mountain to the northwest and a perfect view of Mauna Kea from our backyard to the southeast. When it's clear, the domed observatories sit like giant white marbles delicately placed on the very top of the mountain.

I like to tell people Waimea has to be the only town in the country with more astronomers than homeless people, but when I told a Mendo nice person that, she replied, instructively, "Do you mean astrologers?".

It wasn't until a few weeks ago that my step-daughter Joanie came out from San Francisco to visit, prompting me to take her to the mountain top. We took my 4-wheel drive pick-up, as they won't let any vehicles but 4-wheel or all-wheel drive past the Visitor Center.

Turned out the ranger who last talked to Murphy was off that day, so we joined others waiting by some picnic tables for the scheduled one o'clock caravan to the top, over what turned out to be the worst washboard road ever until the last half-mile of paved road to keep dust down for clearer air for viewing distant stars.

When we got there we saw a few people hanging out by some picnic tables, and just as we sat down some guy starts telling this story about a tourist who left here to hike up the mountain and got lost in a blizzard...I looked at Joanie like wow, unbelievable, after two years the first tourist we meet starts telling the Brian Murphy story. Unable to stop myself, I told the group that I knew that guy...bla bla bla...but I could tell by the way they looked at me they thought I was some big-mouth bull shitter. So I shut up.

When I stopped talking, they turned away and the conversation was over. It was just too far-fetched that after two years a stranger would walk up just at the moment someone starts telling a tale about a missing hiker and claim he knew the guy 40 years ago in Wisconsin.

I wished I'd just kept my mouth shut and listened, but that's another thing I never did very well, except when Brian Murphy was talking.

<u>Postscript:</u> Six years later his skeletal remains were found at the 12,000-foot level, about a mile off the Humuu'ula Trail, suggesting he got lost in the snow. His remains were clothed in a University of Wisconsin-Milwaukee sweatshirt, which made his family quite sure it was him, and the dental records soon confirmed it.

Luck of the Iris

I WAS ON THE SCARY side of 65 when I started noticing newsprint a bit blurry, as if my lens was smudged. So, I'd clean my glasses, thinking these plastic lenses are nice and light, but scratch too easily. I needed real good light to read the smaller print in newspapers and paperbacks, otherwise the blurriness was just an irritating reminder that something was wrong.

I enlarged the font on my computer, and sat closer to the TV, but finally got over my denial when I noticed that my left eye saw clearly when my right eye was closed, but my right eye saw print a bit blurry when my left eye was closed. I finally decided it was time to get a check-up and some new glasses.

I took a *Visual Field Assessment* test, where I'd look into this machine while gripping a lever, and told to push the button whenever I saw a spark, like a shooting star. At first they came slowly, but soon I was pushing that button faster and faster, just like playing a video game. The test-giver kept complimenting my reaction time, so when the test was over I thought I had done pretty well, until she told me that I missed reacting to a "linear line" in the middle of my right eye.

Turned out I not only have glaucoma, but I have already lost vision in my right eye. She showed me a photo of what it looks like behind my eyes. The right eye was redder (bloodier) than the left eye, the results of damaged optic nerve fibers, due to internal pressure within, and hardening of the eyeball, which leads to a gradual impairment of sight, often resulting in blindness…in case you were wondering.

The good news--have you ever noticed no matter how bad a situation is, there's always "good news?" Oh, and you're always "lucky." For example, I don't have the fast-moving glaucoma that occurs from a "sudden blockage, resulting in a rapid pressure build-up, accompanied by blurred vision, colored rings around lights, pain or redness."

Lucky me, I have the slow-moving kind. No hurries, no worries. Chill out, dude. It moves at a casual pace, develops slowly and painlessly, giving me the opportunity to go on enjoying my awesome life…while it gradually destroys my vision without any warning signs. Maybe the first warning sign is denial?

Dr. Kim recommended eye drops to help lower the pressure. I never liked messing with my eyes. Years ago my Willits optometrist told me I was a "bad candidate" for contact lenses because I kept flinching whenever any object came near my eyes. I always preferred to put up with glasses, nerd look and all.

After taking the drops in both eyes every night for two months, I went back to Dr. Kim to see if the eye drops helped. After a painless procedure called *Tonometry*, which measures the internal pressure, she smiled sweetly, telling me that I was lucky because the drops have lowered the pressure from 18 to 14. Sixteen is the norm.

So I asked Dr. Kim, "How long must I take the drops?" But before she could answer, I added, a bit too sarcastically, "The rest of my *life*!" Making *life* sound like, *as if.*

She knocked the smile off my face when she turned from her paper work, looked me in the eyes and said, firmly, "Yes."

I suppose the good news is the rest of my life isn't that fucking long anyhow, what the hell, what's ten, fifteen years? Okay, let's do the math: 10 years is 120 months or 520 weeks or 3,650 days…hmm, maybe that is a long-ish time?

What if I live as long as my grandpa Reinhart? He lived to 92, but was blind from glaucoma the last ten or so years. *The good news is you'll live to 92! The bad news is you'll be blind by the time you're 80.*

I have a clear memory of grandpa sitting in his kitchen chair in the old farm house, next to a large wood burning cook stove, staring straight ahead as if he was seeing something that no one else could see.

I like telling people that my grandpa was alive when President Lincoln was alive. In fact, grandpa Wilhelm Reinhart was born February 28, 1865-- 45 days before Honest Abe was assassinated by John Wilkes Booth.

Since glaucoma is hereditary, I figured if I knew when grandpa Reinhart went blind I'd get an idea how long I had. I was already *over the hill* and picking up speed, so I could not help but wonder.

My older sister Sherry (by five years) does not remember grandpa "ever NOT being blind." Sherry said she remembers mom taking grandpa and us kids on the train to Chicago to have a specialist look at his eyes.

"I remember her holding a toddler in one arm," Sherry does the math in her head—"*that* had to be you—and holding grandpa's arm with the other. I remember we had to wait outside the Men's Room, for what mom called a 'nice man' to come along and help grandpa in the bathroom."

When you need help going to the bathroom, I'd say you're blind. What this means to me is his vision loss had to be severe at the time…that would have been about 1945. He would have been eighty."

That conjured up another memory of grandpa at the old farm house. Since there was no indoor plumbing until the early 50s, he had to go to the outhouse like everybody else, which he did by following a cord someone tied from the back door to the outhouse door—roughly fifty feet away. And he always went alone. Never needed help.

Sherry, by the way, has *Age-related Macular Degeneration* (AMD), which is the leading cause of severe vision loss in people over fifty. There is no cure for either glaucoma or AMD, but the good news is everything is going to hell anyway, and it'll just get worse, so be happy with your beautiful visual memories.

I had another problem. The drops cost $100! And only lasted a month! My tiny *Lumigan 2.5 ml.* vial, containing 0.03% of *Bimatoprost,* is so tiny you can take it on an airplane! That's $1200 per year for eye drops because I don't have Medicare's Plan D.

But the good news: as I rewrite this piece (2-20-12), the generic version, *Latanoprost Ophthalmic Solution,* is now available for just $51! But that's not all! You get three for $51!! Three months worth!!! That's three times more medicine for one-half the price! And you don't have to go to Canada or Mexico or just about any other country in the world for a better deal.

Another interesting read (if I could read print that small) are the side effects: "BIMATOPROST may slowly cause permanent darkening of the eye (iris), eyelid, and eyelashes. Growth and/or thickening of the eyelashes may also occur. This change may not be noticeable for months to several years after starting this medicine."

It sounds a lot like permanent makeup, doesn't it? So these drops enhance a woman's beauty, but what about us guys? The majority of us aren't into the gothic look and don't need longer, thicker eye lashes. Maybe if it somehow smoothed the wrinkles around our eyes or enhanced our virility?

BLIND JOKES

Then I read somewhere that "70% of blind people are unemployed." And my first question was, what do the other 30% do? I told that to a friend and he said, "Answer the phone?"

I've always been a connois-*sewer* of inappropriate humor, but when I asked my friend Noonan if he knew any blind jokes, he replied, without missing a beat, "Why was Helen Keller's leg always yellow?"

Oh man, how could I forget Helen Keller jokes!? That kind of took the wind out of my idea that blind jokes were somehow rare because they were so "inappropriate." Maybe because in my family blind jokes didn't go over too well.

And if you're still reading this and wondering why Ms Keller's leg was always yellow, it was because her dog was blind too. Helen Keller scholar Noonan's deeper research has exposed the fact that Helen Keller was known to masturbate with two hands. Why two hands, you ask? The simple answer of course is she needed one hand to moan.

I asked another friend, how many blind people does it take to change a light bulb? He answered with a question—"Why bother? They're blind!"

Then my second oldest sister Kathy told me she was just diagnosed with glaucoma and also lost vision in her right eye. I'm not sure why I was surprised by that genetic coincidence? It's just that Kathy never wore glasses, never drank alcohol, and never smoked anything... I guess none of that matters when it's part of your genetic make-up.

I think the part that especially bothered me was she lost vision while her pressure wasn't even that high. Just 14, below the 16 level which is considered normal. It made me recall what my Willits optometrist said about glaucoma. To paraphrase, "Glaucoma does whatever the hell it wants to!"

I also asked my cousin Evie, who lives back in central Wisconsin, where most of our clan still reside, and the family farm is located. She reports that three of my mom's seven sisters also had glaucoma, but the good news is they all lived well into their nineties, still had some vision, and were taking eye drops.

In case anyone had any doubt that glaucoma is genetic, only "11% of all blindness and 8% of visual impairment" is due to glaucoma, and it's only the third most common cause of blindness in the U.S. But two of four children in my family is 50%, a bit higher, as is three of nine of my mom's siblings. And Evie is still counting how many glaucoma-diseased cousins and second cousins we have.

After that I forgot about blind humor and started asking people questions like, "If you had to choose between being blind and having no legs, which would it be?" It didn't take long to realize people don't like to think about that kind of stuff, so I pretty much stopped talking about it.

Then I saw a Dennis Miller stand-up routine where he said, "…as high as a Rastafarian with glaucoma." That was funny to me, maybe because I never heard a glaucoma joke before, and now I have it.

Again, I was lucky, because glaucoma is high on the list of legitimate medical reasons for smoking marijuana. The THC in cannabis helps reduce eye pressure, the main cause of retinal damage. And I had been living in Mendocino County, part of the marijuana producing "Emerald Triangle," for most of my adult life. I knew enough people to know who grows and is willing to trade some medicinal herb for, let's say, fresh, cage-free eggs or ripened-on-the-vine tomatoes… or even money.

I didn't like the idea of taking drops every night for the rest of my life, but I did want to slow down the side effects. I decided I would experiment before my next appointment in two months by taking the drops every other night and smoking pot every day!

The problem was I spend my winters in Hawaii (boo hoo) and didn't know any growers there. But I soon hooked up, although the price was rather steep at $300 per ounce! Not to mention how tough it was to make that ounce last for two months.

To make a long, self-incriminating story short, I returned to Dr. Kim only to find an even sweeter smile, saying not only have I not lost any more vision, but my pressure dropped to 13. Then her smile turned less sweet when I told her about my every-other-day eye drop experiment—and that I smoked pot every day! When I asked her opinion if she thought the cannabis helped reduce the pressure, her reaction was, "Don't ask me for a medical marijuana recommendation."

I couldn't help but feel that I could be right, that my experiment showed I didn't need the drops every night. And could it be that pot actually helps? Who would have thunk it?

<u>Postscript</u>: *Five years later I'm still taking eye drops and smoking the medicinal herb, and have not lost anymore vision.*

At Seventy

I learned the truth at seventy
That Medicare was made for me
A simple single-payer plan
That helps us old folks in this land

But many meds they say we need
Have side effects *hard* to believe
From trouble breathing when you sleep
To hard-ons that you keep and keep...at 70!

At seventy I learned the truth
That I am old and long in tooth
I used to run but now I jog
I used to write but now I blog

It's like the world's been rearranged
What once was normal now seems strange
With people even more deranged
I used to care but things have changed

I learned the truth at seventy
That marijuana's good for me
It lowers pressure in my eye
And did I mention I get high...at 70

I learned some priests like little boys
They use their penises for toys
And if they're caught they move away
To PREY again another day

I learned that global warming's real
That man must help the earth to heal
But since the end is looming near
We might as well have one more beer…at 70

***Postscript:** I was approaching 70 when I heard this old Janis Ian hit from 1974, AT SEVENTEEN, and wondered if she could use another hit? Maybe her next hit could be AT SEVENTY. It didn't take long for the above lyrics to spew forth.*

ACKNOWLEDGEMENTS

I WOULD LIKE TO THANK Maggie Siegfried for the drawings she did back in 1972. They sat at Ed Burton's place in Milwaukee until 2015, when his widow, Vickie, found them and sent them to me. Thanks Vickie.

I'd also like to thank Bruce Anderson, editor of the *Anderson Valley Advertiser* {theava.com} whose support is a big reason this book is finally completed. Many of these stories were first published in his weekly newspaper over the last few years, but some go way back to the 80s.

I should also thank the Sausalito Historical Society for the images of Alan Watts and Jean Varda in their fascinating book, *Images of America: Sausalito*. This is a must read for anyone living in Northern California, and can be ordered online at bookpassage.com.

More recently, my experience at weekly meetings with other Hawaii Writers Guild members has helped me with final editing and inspired me to get it done. You can find us at hawaiiwritersguild.com, Facebook, and Twitter.

Many of these poems and essays were first published in:

Brewing: 20 Milwaukee Poets, the Giglia Press c.1972

Frida: A Cultural Revolution Magazine

Garlic Press, a small newsletter out of Gate 6 (defunct)

Marin Scope, Sausalito

Mendocino County Grapevine (defunct)

New Settler Magazine, Mendocino County

Poems Here and Now, Greenwillow Press c.1976

Prime the Pump, Morgan Press c.1970

Hey Lady, Morgan Press (defunct)

The Suspicious Humanist, c.1970 (defunct)

The Willits News

ABOUT THE AUTHOR

JIM GIBBONS' WRITING CAREER STARTED
his junior year in high school when he
made the wrestling team, but noticed his
school newspaper didn't cover the team's
recent victories. He complained to the
editor, who countered, "Do *you* wanna
do it?" Gibbons did it, and became sports
editor the following year.

A similar thing happened when he was
on the wrestling team at the University of
Wisconsin-Milwaukee, except he didn't
become sports editor, but took a poetry
class with Barbara Gibson and became a well-known Milwaukee poet,
printing a small local poetry magazine called *Pretty Mama*, and giving
readings with other Milwaukee Poets at the *Avant Garde* coffee house.

Gibbons' first book of poems, *Prime the Pump*, was the first book
printed by Morgan Press in 1970. Ed Burton's Morgan Press, operated
from his Milwaukee basement, went on to print many more creative poetry
books, chapbooks, posters, and postcards.

Gibbons' poetry was included in newspapers, magazines, and poetry
anthologies with some of his favorite poets, including Richard Brautigan,
Charles Bukowski, Gregory Corso, Lawrence Ferlinghetti, Frank O'Hara,

Jack Kerouac, Anne Sexton, Lew Welch, Phillip Whalen, William Carlos Williams, and Al Young.

However, before he was published with his poetry heroes, he had turned his back on the poetry scene by dropping out and moving to the woods of Mendocino County in Northern California, where he built funky cabins and helped raise his two boys.

In the late 70s, Gibbons went back to school to get his teaching credential, and got into running. He returned to journalism and wrote a weekly running column for the *Willits News* called *FootNotes,* and briefly became the *Willits News* sports editor. He also taught at three different schools in the local school district, and coached the runners at the high school.

His next book, *Going for the Bronze,* will be a collection of articles he wrote for the *Willits News* and the *Anderson Valley Advertiser* about his experience travelling to different races across the country, from Buffalo to Boston to Miami to San Francisco, and finally retiring in Hawaii, where this memoir was written.